P9-DMA-282

❝ As the American family continues to struggle and break down, the children absorb much of the pain and confusion from living in a culture that values success and appearance over character and integrity. Girls in particular need guidance and wisdom in finding out who they really are beyond their boyfriends or social cliques. *Salvaging My Identity* is filled with practical, common sense truth that every American girl needs to make it in this culture. Grounded in biblical truth, it's a powerful resource for young women who struggle with their identity, their insecurities, and the fears that come along with being young and unsure of the future. ❞

CLAYTON KING *President, Crossroads Ministries / Teaching Pastor, NewSpring Church / Campus Pastor, Liberty University*

❝ Allow me to recommend this instant classic, *Salvaging My Identity* by Jennifer Mills and Rachel Lovingood! Like a cool drink of water on a hot summer day, this book is a refreshing approach for young ladies growing into adulthood. I am not only a speaker to teens, but also a father to a teenage girl. I am indebted to you for giving people like me a tool so effective for young ladies. Every young lady would be challenged, inspired, and encouraged by reading this book. ❞

SCOTT DAWSON *www.ScottDawson.org*

❝ The hyper-sexualized bandit of commercialism has robbed young girls of their identity today. The crime scene is heartbreaking. Stripped of their self worth, honor, and purpose girls are left cluelessly stuck in a deadly game of identity charades. *Salvaging My Identity* is a game changer! Jennifer Mills & Rachel Lovingood have broken through the madness and the guessing is over! Each sentence and every chapter brings high definition clarity, rescuing girls from a life of painful pantomimes to one of stability, value, and power. ❞

TONY NOLAN *Author / Evangelist*

❝ With the opening definition of the word "salvaged" my heart knew *Salvaging My Identity* is a rescue for this generation of young women. It is biblically rich and culturally astute, while challenging girls to "re-think" critical topics such as image obsession, failure, shame, and a host of others. This is a bold work and desperately needed. Women of all ages, read this book and engage a younger woman—you may help salvage her identity. ❞

KATHY FERGUSON LITTON *National Consultant for Ministry to Pastor's Wives at NAMB*

❝ As a woman whose life's work has been pouring into high school and college students, being a mom of two young adult women and aunt to eight girls ranging from 5-15, I see DAILY how crucial the message of *Salvaging My Identity* is. This next generation of girls desperately needs to understand and walk in their true identity that is in Christ and Christ alone! In a world that is constantly bombarding girls with lies and impossible expectations, this book is a must-read guide as well as an authentic reminder that we are all, no matter our age, searching to know our true identity. Rachel and Jennifer bring a fresh and realistic perspective to this hot topic that is applicable to girls and young women of today. ❞

KRISTI MALZAHN *Wife of Gus Malzahn, Auburn University Head Football Coach*

❝ Excellent. Engaging. Spoken into the heart of this generation in honest, strong biblical truth. *Salvaging My Identity* will challenge and encourage young ladies to incorporate God's truth in daily living as they salvage their identity in Christ Jesus. Written for a small group or individually...A much needed book for young women! ❞

ESTHER BURROUGHS *Author, Speaker, Bible Teacher*

❝ This book is a refreshing and powerful resource for young women who are already struggling against succumbing to the lies of this age regarding identity and character. Through their eight "projects," Rachel and Jennifer contrast biblical truth with cultural values and guide the reader toward understanding God's highest and best plan for her. Specifically written for young women, this book delivers! ❞

SUSIE HAWKINS *Bible Study teacher / Flourish writing team / www.flourish.me*

❝ Relevant, life changing, and foundational, this journey will give young women direction and result in exponential spiritual growth. Every young woman needs this book! ❞

JEANA FLOYD *Wife of Dr. Ronnie Floyd, Senior Pastor of Cross Church, Northwest AR*

RACHEL LOVINGOOD & JENNIFER MILLS

salvaging MY IDENTITY

A 40 DAY EXPERIENCE FOR GIRLS & YOUNG WOMEN

LIFEWAY PRESS®
NASHVILLE, TENNESSEE

© 2013 LifeWay Press®

No part of this work may be reproduced or transmitted in any form or by any means, electronic or mechanical, including photocopying and recording, or by any information storage or retrieval system, except as may be expressly permitted in writing by the publisher.

Requests for permission should be addressed in writing to LifeWay Press®, One LifeWay Plaza, Nashville, TN 37234-0144.

ISBN: 978-1-4300-3248-9
Item Number: 005647983

Dewey Decimal Classification Number: 248.843
Subject Heading: GIRLS \ SPIRITUAL LIFE \ CHRISTIAN LIFE

Printed in the United States of America

We believe that the Bible has God for its author; salvation for its end; and truth, without any mixture of error, for its matter and that all Scripture is totally true and trustworthy. To review LifeWay's doctrinal guideline, please visit *www.lifeway.com/doctrinalguideline.*

Scripture Copyright © 1999, 2000, 2002, 2003, 2009 by Holman Bible Publishers. Used by permission. Holman Christian Standard Bible® and HCSB® are federally registered trademarks of Holman Bible Publishers.

Scripture quotations marked ESV are from The Holy Bible, English Standard Version® (ESV®), copyright © 2001 by Crossway, a publishing ministry of Good News Publishers. Used by permission. All rights reserved.

Scripture quotations marked NIV are from the Holy Bible, New International Version, copyright © 1973, 1978, 1984 by International Bible Society.

Scripture quotations marked (NLT) are taken from the Holy Bible, New Living Translation, copyright © 1996. Used by permission of Tyndale House Publishers, Inc., Wheaton, IL 60189 USA. All rights reserved.

From the New King James Bible—New Testament. Copyright © 1979, 1982, Thomas Nelson, Inc., Publishers.

Student Ministry Publishing
LifeWay Church Resources
One LifeWay Plaza
Nashville, TN 37234-0144

Cover photo: Jennifer Wingate, *PhotoJENic Photography* (Auburn, AL)

Table of Contents

RACHEL LOVINGOOD

Rachel is a wife, mom, author, and speaker. She is married to Jeff, Pastor of the Next Generation at Long Hollow Baptist Church. They have two young adult children and one high schooler. Over the past 26 years of marriage and ministry, Rachel has developed a passion to see people get in God's Word to experience true life change. She has written curriculum for years and recently started Impact Resources that offers strong, biblically-based resources for students and adults.

JENNIFER MILLS

Jennifer is the wife of Student Pastor, Brian Mills, and mom to McKenna and Parker. She is a speaker who has a heart for teaching God's Word and is actively serving at Long Hollow Baptist Church in Hendersonville, TN where she is heavily involved in girls' and women's ministry. Jennifer has a passion for girls' ministry and in investing in this generation. Through communicating the truth from God's Word, her heart's desire is to see girls and young women find their identity in Christ and to discover a passion for the God who has pursued and redeemed them.

Special thanks...

A project like this has so many people to thank. We want to start with our husbands, Jeff Lovingood and Brian Mills. The privilege of leading together in ministry is indescribable, and we are grateful you have brought us along on this journey. Thanks also to our kids Trevor, Kelsey, and Riley Lovingood and McKenna and Parker Mills. We love being your moms and you have taught us so much about life and love and who we are.

This started as a project for the girls at our church, and we are thankful to LifeWay for seeing the vision of what it can be to girls and young women everywhere. Thanks for giving us the opportunity to let the work that God ordained in us spread to so many more. Our passion is for girls and women to live the way God designed them to—in freedom and abundance, secure in who they are in Christ. Alicia Claxton is a rockstar to us as she has poured herself into the editing and formatting while keeping our voice and passion consistent and clear—we love you girl! Thanks Mike Wakefield, Jeff Pratt, and Ben Trueblood and all those involved in helping bring this project to life.

Special thanks to our sweet friend Alexa Follas for giving us her insight from a Christian counseling perspective and sharing her thoughts in Healing Brokenness. Alexa you are such a special gift from God, and we are grateful for your godly insight, spiritual wisdom, friendship, and your heart for girls and young women. You take these topics to another level in our quest to bring healing to broken areas. We love you.

To the student ministry and staff at Long Hollow Baptist Church. You have given us the opportunity to do life with you, and we will never take that for granted.

Special thanks to Carson Oakley and Macy Tollett for sharing your real life perspectives.

Special thanks to Livi and Company in Albany, GA, for the use of the beautiful desk by "Eddie Lee's Stuff" seen in the cover image.

Dear Friend,

By definition, to salvage something is to save it from loss or destruction and restore its beauty and usefulness. Let's face it, we are living in a day and age where the enemy is wreaking havoc on the hearts and minds of young women. Our culture entices us to focus on ALL the wrong things and if not tackled head-on can leave us in quite the predicament as a girl, of any age, striving to live a godly life. The reason we sat down to write this book was to give young women a practical guide to get into the Word, dig for TRUTH, and find out just what God intends for those who love Him. We also wanted to give you action steps to take on the journey of SALVAGING your identity in Christ!

We are fed lies on a daily basis about what we need to wear, do, look like, and act like—none of which are what Christ intends for us to chase after in order to achieve the abundant, fulfilling life that He desires for us. Our hearts break at the reality that we live in a world where there is so much hurt, pain, unforgiveness, and abuse!

Our prayer for you as you walk through this 40 day journey comes straight from Colossians 1:9-14 (HCSB): "For this reason also, since the day we heard this, we haven't stopped praying for you. We are asking that you may be filled with the knowledge of His will in all wisdom and spiritual understanding, so that you may walk worthy of the Lord, fully pleasing to Him, bearing fruit in every good work and growing in the knowledge of God. May you be strengthened with all power, according to His glorious might, for all endurance and patience, with joy giving thanks to the Father, who has enabled you to share in the saints' inheritance in the light. He has rescued us from the domain of darkness and transferred us into the kingdom of the Son He loves. We have redemption, the forgiveness of sins, in Him."

Sincerely,

Rachel & Jennifer

HOW TO...

A good salvaging project comes with some "how to" tips. The following pages will help you get the most out of this book by highlighting the different features and giving you some "how to" steps. Read through these FAQs then get started on your first project!

Q :: What is this book about?

A :: To "salvage" something is to save it from loss or destruction and restore its beauty and usefulness. This book is a 40 day experience about growth, confession, brokenness, and restoration. Even if you've made mistakes in the past, it's about forgetting what's behind and striving for what's ahead...opening your heart and mind to the transformation that takes place through Jesus Christ!

Q :: Why are the chapter titles called "Projects"?

A :: When you salvage something, you invest time and energy into a project of restoration. We are all at different places in our spiritual journeys but there are some common issues we face. We're going to look at 8 "projects" that represent areas of growth you must seek in order to salvage your identity.

Q :: What kind of "Junk" will we be dealing with in this experience?

A :: Each day we are going to hash out some "junk" that might be hindering you from fully living the life God created you for! We will deal with issues that every young woman can relate to on some level. Check out the table of contents for the full list of Projects and Junk we will work through over the next 40 days.

Q :: What should I expect from this experience?

A :: You should expect the Lord to do great things in you over the next 40 days. Getting the most out of this experience will require an investment of time, honesty, and openness on your part. The reward will be the freedom you will feel as you and Jesus strip away the junk in your life!

Q :: What does "DIY" mean?

A :: At the end of each day will be a "DIY" (Do It Yourself) section that will give you some action steps you need to take. It's DIY because it has to be your choice and no one else can do it for you. Through journaling, Scripture memory, personal evaluation, and prayer time each day you can move forward in the process of taking back what the enemy has tried to steal.

Q :: Is there a place for me to write answers or journal my prayers as I go through this journey?

A :: YES! There are plenty of journal pages in the back of the book (starting on page 174) for that purpose. Fill those pages with thoughts, Scripture, and prayers. These pages will be a written reminder of what you've learned and how the Lord has worked in you during this experience!

Q :: What is the "Healing Brokenness" section and why is it only found on certain days?

A :: We feel like some of the "junk" we deal with in this book may require a deeper look into the issues at hand. In Healing Brokenness, you will find information and guidance to help you wrestle more effectively with these particularly difficult issues.

Q :: Do I need to go through this book on my own or with a group?

A :: It is designed for you to read on your own, but you will get even more out of this experience if you walk through it with an accountability partner, mentor, best friend, or small group. Beginning on page 168 you will find a section called Re-Hash for those who want to lead this as a small group study. It includes additional illustrations and questions to discuss in a weekly setting.

PROJECT:

Rescue Identity

He has rescued us from the domain of darkness and transferred us into the kingdom of the Son He loves. We have redemption, the forgiveness of sins, in Him.
Colossians 1:13-14 (HCSB)

Have you ever been out in the ocean and felt like you were being carried away? Recently a breaking news story told the tale of supermodel Heidi Klum who raced into the ocean to save her son and his nanny from a riptide. Apparently a big wave washed in and started pulling them out away from the safety of shore. Heidi wasted no time jumping in to help rescue her loved ones.

It can happen slowly or suddenly. You are enjoying the waves, maybe floating on something, then all of a sudden you realize the shore is very far away. It can be a very dangerous and scary time. All the stories of situations like these don't have happy endings like Heidi's rescue did. In an interview afterwards Heidi said that she just did what any mother would do when she sees her son in trouble. She also said, "Never underestimate the power of the ocean."

That's a great statement and exactly what we want to get you thinking about today. Many girls just like you are floating along in the waters of the world, not really realizing they are being sucked out into a place where they are in need of rescue. Like them, your identity is being washed away wave after wave until you are struggling with figuring out who you really are. Now is the time for you to call out to God and join Him in rescuing your identity!

These next five days we'll look at some of the biggest obstacles you will need to overcome in order to execute an identity rescue. These obstacles represent the "junk" that needs to be dealt with so you can shine through and reveal the treasure you were designed to be.

Be encouraged—you are not alone and the very One who created you will enable you to jump into the fray and fight through the waves. Don't underestimate the power of the ocean. More importantly, don't underestimate the infinite power of your God!

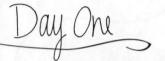

JUNK: ACCEPTANCE

> For am I now trying to win the favor of people, or God? Or am I striving to please people? If I were still trying to please people, I would not be a slave of Christ. **Galatians 1:10** (HCSB)

Let's be honest, as a girl the desire for acceptance and approval will never change no matter if you're 9 or 90. Maybe there is some magical age when you actually stop caring about what people think about you...but I'm definitely not there yet!

+ "Will they like me?"
+ "I need to do this with him so he won't leave me."
+ "Were they talking about me?"
+ "Did they think I was funny?"
+ "Will I make friends when I walk into this new class?"
+ "I'll just drink one drink so I won't look like a complete loser."
+ "Does he think I'm beautiful?"

These crazy questions, and others like them, plague our minds on a daily basis as we seek the approval of people in the world we live in. As girls, we're so stinkin' analytical that we drive ourselves crazy wondering if we're good enough or if we're measuring up. We are willing to compromise who we are and what we believe, all for the approval of people, both guys and other girls! Why?!

A girl in our student ministry posted this online, and I challenge you with this thought: "We often lose sight of Jesus when we are with others. Our fear of displeasing people puts us in bondage to them and they then become our focus." Such a strong word, right?! Have you ever sat back and thought, why do I put myself through this torture of being desperate to be accepted and validated by all these people whose opinions change like the wind? Why am I willing to compromise my convictions and who I truly am at any cost? Why do I fear displeasing people over displeasing God?

The need for acceptance is a poison that seeps into our thoughts and becomes an obsession, which eventually becomes toxic to our spiritual lives. The enemy is super crafty and knows what makes us "tick." He knows just the right buttons to push to drive us further into that dark place in our thoughts and further away from the light and truth of God's Word. The truth of the matter is, it's not about who we can impress or what we can achieve—it's about Jesus. Through His finished work on the cross, those who trust in Him are completely accepted!

Galatians 1:10 says, "For am I now trying to win the favor of people, or God? Or am I striving to please people? If I were still trying to please people, I would not be a slave of Christ."

When we become completely focused on the acceptance of others, it's all consuming and we lose sight of the fact that our Creator has accepted us completely in Christ! He sees the good, the bad, and the ugly and still loves us! If you open your heart and allow the Lord to validate you through His Spirit, you will begin to see yourself the way He sees you. The approval of people will then fade into the background, and you will no longer obsess over what people think about you or whether you measure up to a false expectation from an unrealistic culture. And it's then that you will discover the abundant life promised to you from your loving, gracious God.

God knows you, loves you, and fully accepts you—the real you. In order for you to reclaim your identity you need to start by knowing yourself. Turn to the journal pages (p.174) in the back of this book and draw a stick figure representing you. Be as creative as you want. Once you are on the page, list some things that honestly describe you right now such as: insecure, scared, happy, depressed, anxious, stressed, joyful, worthless, funny, reliable, mean, gossipy, wimpy, strong, guilty, failure, or anything else that comes to mind when you think of who you really are. No one else will see this so be completely honest. It is just between you and the Lord.

DIY:

Re-Think (Journal & Pray):

+ Ask the Lord to show you areas of your life where you are compromising who you are and who you desire to be. What's standing in your way? What areas of acceptance/approval do you struggle in the most? Boys? Friends? Popularity? Even seeking God's approval by trying to DO good things?
+ Confession time is key to breaking free from your sin and selfishness and growing up in your walk with Christ. He doesn't desire for you to live a life that is bogged down and heavy—caught up in what everyone else thinks of you!
+ Ask Him to help you find freedom from an obsession with acceptance.

Re-Visit the Word:

+ Galatians 1:10
+ Colossians 3:23
+ John 10:10

Re-Claim:

Get an accountability partner, someone you can have "real talk" with. Share your insecurities and struggles with her. If people at school, church, or your teammates are pulling you down because of your desire for acceptance from them, ask her to pray with you about finding an amazing group of friends who love Jesus. Encourage one another. Pray for one another to find true joy, contentment, approval, and self-worth in Jesus!

JUNK: APPEARANCE/IMAGE OBSESSION

> Give to the LORD the glory due His name; Bring an offering, and come before Him. Oh, worship the LORD in the beauty of holiness! **1 Chronicles 16:29** (NKJV)

When was the last time you felt beautiful? When you look in the mirror do you have positive thoughts or negative thoughts? The majority of us spend so much of our time comparing ourselves to the wrong kinds of models and standards that it is virtually impossible to have a healthy view of ourselves. Anytime we try to live up to a standard of beauty based on the world's definition, we WILL end up discouraged and disillusioned.

But there's a deeper meaning to this concept of beauty. The truth is that even on your bad hair, face broken out, worst day, you are still beautiful in God's eyes. The secret is found in how you respond to the awesomeness of God. Scripture says in 1 Chronicles 16:29, "Give to the LORD the glory due His name; Bring an offering, and come before Him. Oh, worship the LORD in the beauty of holiness!"

That, girlfriends, is the key to your beauty. When you honor the Lord—you are being holy—holiness is beautiful! Instead of basing your beauty on impossible standards that a crazy world sets, true beauty can be found in holiness and choosing to set your standards based on the Word of God. Let's face it. The standards of the world are actually working against the purposes of God for us. When you seek after what the world dictates about the size of your waist, weight on the scale, or anything else on your body, you are listening to the wrong voices, and you will never find the satisfaction that you crave.

Consider the pictures you see in magazines or Instagram or wherever that you hold up as goals for your physical appearance. Do they look like holiness? Or are they all about exploiting the body and using it to achieve power of some kind? When the goal is to get people to notice your body and be impressed, you are obsessed with the wrong things and God will not honor that. You may get the world's attention, but you will miss the very purpose for which you were created—to bring God glory with every part of your life. There will also be other consequences we will talk about in upcoming topics. So—what do you need to do to start this process of rescuing your identity? Walk through the DIY section, be honest, and allow the Lord to change your attitude and focus. After all, He is the One who defines beauty!

DIY:

Re-Think (Journal & Pray):

+ On a scale of 1-10 where would you be if 1 is "don't even think about my appearance" and 10 is "obsessed with my appearance"?
+ Most of us don't think we are obsessed with our appearance and image (because we know we aren't supposed to be), but the truth comes out when we answer these questions: How much time do you spend getting ready each day? How much time do you spend talking about your looks? (hair, skin, body, weight, size, etc.) Can your day be ruined by how you look?
+ Compare your previous answers to these questions that indicate focus on true beauty: How much time do you spend daily in prayer and the Word of God? Are you more concerned that people recognize you as a Christian or that they are impressed with your looks?
+ Pray and confess any misguided focus and obsession you may have. Ask God to help you care more about being who He wants you to be rather than how you look. That is when you will truly start to be more beautiful than you ever could have imagined...

and that's not just to God—because true beauty will shine through you, and other people will notice the difference!
+ Read 1 Peter 1:13-16 and pray that God will show you how to be holy like He is holy. Then listen to the Holy Spirit as He reveals things to you about the beauty of holiness.

Re-Visit the Word:

+ 1 Chronicles 16:29
+ 1 Peter 1:13-16

Re-Claim:

In small group or with your accountability partner, agree to call each other out when you talk about your appearance too much. Be intentional about spending more time focused on your spiritual life than your physical appearance—instead of stress and anxiety, you will be living with peace and love. That's enough to make you more beautiful right there!

HEALING BROKENNESS:

Today we are talking about having a healthy body image and a good self-esteem! Both of these topics are very important when it comes to young women. How far is too far though? When does obsessing over our bodies, watching what we eat, and thinking about our appearance become a problem? And what do we to do if we or someone we know is suffering with more than just a negative self-image? Well, here are a few important facts to know:
+ Studies show that over half of teen girls and one third of teen boys use unhealthy weight control behaviors such as skipping meals, fasting, smoking, vomiting, or taking laxatives to maintain weight.
+ Anorexia is the third most common chronic illness among adolescents.[1]

It might be time to ask yourself or your friend a few of the following questions:

+ Do you constantly find yourself looking in the mirror and thinking you are "fatter" than you are actually are?
+ Do you starve yourself?
+ Do you often eat in secret?
+ Does your weight affect the way you feel about yourself?
+ Do you make yourself sick because you feel uncomfortably full?
+ Do you worry you have lost control over how much you eat?
+ Would you say that food dominates your life?

If you find yourself answering yes to most of these questions, or you know someone who might struggle with an eating disorder, it is time to ask for help! First of all, it is important to understand that eating disorders are often caused by a lack of control in one's life. When someone feels she has several circumstances she cannot control, she may turn to food, which is something she can control in order to better manage her emotions. This is very damaging in the long term and can lead to a more serious illness. Triggers for eating disorders include certain abuse early on, certain athletic involvements, traumatic experiences, difficult periods of adjustment, etc.

Helpful tips include:
+ Managing stress
+ Eating three meals a day plus snacks
+ Exercising
+ Fighting boredom
+ Listening to your body
+ Most of all, getting support

Reaching out to a friend, parent, teacher, counselor, or pastor is a great way to get on the right track to healing brokenness in regard to your self-image. Begin the process of rescuing your identity to be in line with who God created you to be.

JUNK: FAILURE/SHAME

Therefore, no condemnation now exists for those in Christ Jesus. **Romans 8:1** (HCSB)

Can I just begin today by giving you a very freeing thought? NO ONE has it all together! Some of you reading this really need to hear that. I absolutely love this quote by Pastor Steven Furtick of Elevation Church, "The reason we struggle with insecurity is because we compare our behind-the-scenes with everyone else's highlight reel."

In this day of social media, people are daily putting their "best foot forward"...no one is out there putting a status update about their mistakes and failures or uploading pictures of their acne and bad hair days. We tend to look at other girls and think they've got it all figured out and they've never made bad choices in their lives. Yet, in reality we're all sinners in need of a Savior. We have all made choices in our lives that we're not proud of and if not dealt with will leave us feeling shameful and isolated.

In Philippians 3:13-14, Paul reminds us that NONE of us has it all together: "No, dear brothers and sisters, I have not achieved it, but I focus on this one thing: Forgetting the past and looking forward to what lies ahead, I press on to reach the end of the race and receive the heavenly prize for which God, through Christ Jesus, is calling us" (NLT).

We've all had those moments in our lives where we said the wrong thing, were at the wrong place at the wrong time, or did things we're not proud of. Does God require perfection from us? No, He knows we cannot attain that on our own. That's why Jesus had to come to redeem and achieve salvation for us. But what God does require from us is holiness, godliness, and growth in living out lives that are fully surrendered to Him.

We've got to keep striving for what's ahead! We can't let the enemy keep reminding us on a daily basis that we're a failure because of our past mistakes. We must keep moving forward through this life and not let our past define who we are. Living this life out as a follower of Christ isn't easy and none of us has it all figured out. Yet so many believers miss out on the freedom that is offered through Christ. He desires for us to open our hearts and let Him write a beautiful story with our lives. He can even use our flaws and failures for a greater purpose.

DIY:

Re-Think (Journal & Pray):

+ Take some time alone, just you and the Lord, to revisit your past.
+ Are there areas of unconfessed sin in your life that the enemy is using to define you? What's holding you back from freedom or from where God wants you to go? Spend this time of prayer before a God that loves you and has a perfect plan for your life— flaws, mistakes, and all.

Re-Visit the Word:

+ Memorize: Philippians 3:13-14
+ Romans 8:1
+ Psalm 34

Re-Claim:

In small group or with your accountability partner, discuss ways that the Lord wants to free you from past decisions and the shame and guilt that you've been carrying!

HEALING BROKENNESS:

Based on research, there is a profound difference between shame and guilt. It is important to remember that "Godly sorrow brings repentance that leads to salvation and leaves no regret, but worldly sorrow brings spiritual death" (2 Cor. 7:10, NIV). Guilt can be a good thing when it causes us to change our negative behaviors and move in a different direction; however, shame goes deeper and affects how we view ourselves.

Dr. Brené Brown is a research professor making groundbreaking discoveries in the healing of shame, and she defines shame as: an intensely painful feeling or experience that leaves us feeling as if we are flawed and therefore, unworthy of love and belonging.[2] Shame is paralyzing and can keep us from ever fully taking hold of all that God has for us because we feel we do not deserve it. It can leave us feeling as though God made a mistake when He made us and there is no chance we can change.

If you find yourself replaying these thoughts in your mind, you may have hidden shame you need to deal with...

+ I am not important.
+ I am a failure.
+ I am not worthy of love or anything good.
+ I am unlovable.
+ Something is wrong with me.

First and foremost, these thoughts are not true and do not line up with the Word of God and who He says you are. One of the best ways to heal shame is to admit that this is something you are struggling with. You are not alone. Many people, especially young women, struggle with shame. It is important that you reach out for help and find someone you can trust to talk to. Shame is best healed by being vulnerable with what you are experiencing and being met in your place of weakness with unconditional love, grace, and acceptance.

Remember that God loves you just the way you are, and you are His princess. He has redeemed you through the blood of Christ and forgiven your sins. He loves you and has a purpose and plan for your life. God makes no mistakes. It is time to let go of shame, talk about your feelings so they lose their power, and most of all realize you are important and loved!

JUNK: DISCONTENTMENT

> Get rid of all bitterness, rage and anger, brawling and slander, along with every form of malice. Be kind and compassionate to one another, forgiving each other, just as in Christ God forgave you. **Ephesians 4:31-32** (NIV)

Do you ever get tired of the competition? Not in athletics but the competition between you and your friends and even those you wouldn't call friends? It seems as if we are being caught up in this race to have everything better and nicer than anyone else, and it's causing serious problems. When you look at Facebook or Instagram are you usually happy and enjoying what you see, or does it make you more discontent and longing to be someone else or have what she has?

This world is always telling us that we "deserve more" and not to settle for what we have but to keep on trying to get more and get ahead of everyone else. It can be a real problem when it translates into our relationships and affects our walk with the Lord. Think about all the things that discontentment does to you. It makes you secretly happy when something bad happens to someone else, from getting a zit on prom day to her boyfriend breaking up with her. Because after all—her life is so perfect that maybe now she can understand what it's like to be normal like you. Ummm, do you see a problem with that line of thinking?!

Nowhere in the Word of God are we told to rejoice or be happy when bad things happen to other people, but that's what discontentment does.

Discontentment also makes us long for more than what we have—even if we have to get it at someone else's expense. After all, we deserve at least as much as she does. Right? Wrong—that's also not from God. Sometimes life doesn't seem fair. Sometimes other people have more money, better clothes, cooler parents, nicer cars, and other better things than we do. That's just the way it is. When you live with discontentment, you miss out on all the things that God wants to do in you and through your circumstances. He may have chosen you to reach people for the gospel because of what you have gone through in your life and how you have learned "to be content in any and every situation" like the apostle Paul said in Philippians 4:12-13: "I know what it is to be in need, and I know what it is to have plenty. I have learned the secret of being content in any and every situation, whether well fed or hungry, whether living in plenty or in want. I can do everything through him who gives me strength" (NIV). Yes. That's a verse often quoted about playing harder or doing better on a test, but read it in its context, you will see that it really has to do with being CONTENT. By the way, the struggles that Paul faced were a little heavier than our normal concerns. He was talking about being in prison, beaten, stoned, shipwrecked, and that kind of stuff. If he can say with confidence that he learned the secret of contentment then maybe we should apply that same attitude to our lives.

DIY:

Re-Think (Journal & Pray):

+ What are you discontent about in your life?
+ How have you seen discontentment lead you into sin? (wrong attitude, negative thoughts and words, etc.)
+ Confess the things He has revealed to you and thank Him for forgiving you. Remember that repenting is about stopping and turning from the sin. Ask the Lord to convict you just before you give in to the sin of discontentment next time and deal with it quickly.

Re-Visit the Word:

+ Philippians 4:12-13

Re-Claim:

In small group or with your accountability partner, memorize Philippians 4:13. Remember when you think about it or hear it that it is really based on being content with what you have and where you are. Look around and see your circumstances as what they really are: an opportunity for God to use you to make a difference and IMPACT the world with the gospel!

Day Five

JUNK: FALSE EXPECTATIONS

No eye has seen, no ear has heard, and no mind has imagined what God has prepared for those who love him. **1 Corinthians 2:9** (NLT)

We live in a fairytale-driven world. There are tons of movies, books, and television shows that end in "happily ever after." If we aren't careful, we can begin to romanticize our lives and base our expectations on fictional stories that move us.

Just look at the entertainment industry and the fantasy world it has created. Young and old, we are inundated today with romantic comedies, steamy novels, and beautifully scripted love stories played out on screen. Now, don't get me wrong. I'm the first girl to want to run out and see the latest "chick flick." The problem creeps in when we begin to dream about these "stories," expecting them to play out in our reality like they do on screen or in a novel.

Obviously, there are other ways that false expectations can affect our outlook on our lives aside from how the entertainment world affects us. You can always uncover any false expectations in your own life when you step back and look at what your reaction is when something doesn't work out the way you think it should. False expectations feed our sense of entitlement. When you begin to measure your identity based on what you're "getting" out of life, that's when your identity becomes clouded and questionable. These false expectations leave you feeling disappointed, empty,

27

and unsatisfied, only wanting more or the next best thing. When you focus on those things, you will miss out on the BEST thing— God's plan and purpose for your life. God never promises that life will be all daisies and roses. In fact, life is hard, love is hard, and we live in a fallen world. That is our reality. But girls, you are loved and pursued by a loving, gracious Savior, who loves it when you depend on Him for realistic guidance, clear direction, and dream with Him!

1 Corinthians 2:9 says, "No eye has seen, no ear has heard, and no mind has imagined what God has prepared for those who love him."

You can't even imagine what the Lord, who loves you and created you, has prepared for your life! Notice that Paul uses the word "prepared" in this passage. It's past tense because it's already been done. When you allow false expectations to fuel what you strive for in life, you short yourselves of God's divine plan and purpose that He has already prepared for you. His Word says you can't even begin to IMAGINE what that purpose looks like.

DIY:

Re-Think (Journal & Pray):

+ What are some areas of your life where you are struggling with some false expectations? Do you struggle with entitlement? Expecting people to do what you want? For things to go your way, or else? How have movies, books, friends, or other things in our culture affected your view on life?
+ Confess to the Lord for believing in and pursuing the lies from our culture rather than DESIRING His best plan and purpose for your life.

Re-Visit the Word:

+ Memorize: 1 Corinthians 2:9
+ Ephesians 3:20-21

Re-Claim:

In small group or with your accountability partner, share ways that unrealistic expectations have affected your view on love, marriage, and your future. Do you live a life thinking these unrealistic views are what you deserve?

2

Reclaim Reputation

Keep a close watch on how you live and on your teaching.
Stay true to what is right for the sake of your own
salvation and the salvation of those who hear you.
1 Timothy 4:16 (NLT)

I absolutely love how Paul words his letter to Timothy in 1 Timothy 4:16, that we are to keep a close watch on how we live...staying TRUE to what is RIGHT for the sake of our own salvation and the salvation of those who hear us (our witness). As you make decisions in your life, a lot of hurt and heartache can be avoided if you would only stop and think before you speak, act out, send that text, or upload that picture.

Thanks to social media, we live in a day where we have to be SO CAREFUL about what we are uploading or posting out there about ourselves. Just one night, one choice, one mistake, one drink, one picture, one text sent can absolutely destroy your reputation. So much can be misinterpreted online, and we have got to be pro-active about what we decide to put out there about ourselves. We all know of someone, or maybe that someone is you, that has made that one decision to do, say, or post something that totally jeopardized the girl you once were or the girl you STILL desire to be, and you feel that your reputation has been destroyed.

For example, maybe you've made one choice to do something you regret with some guy. Now you're feeling the failure and shame that comes from that decision, and you've fallen for the lie that you've messed up so this has to be your "new normal." Or everybody else has believed some lie about you that may not be 100 percent true, but you've totally picked up the part and act as if they are right. Maybe you've become real good at playing the part instead of fighting to reclaim the truth of who you are or, more importantly, fighting for who you truly desire to be and who God created you to be.

For you, maybe your problem isn't poor choices with boys. Maybe the problem is your mouth. Are you the "Negative Nancy"? Always focused on the negative in life to the point that it absolutely drains everyone around you.

Or you might be the biggest gossip in your entire school or student ministry. Your mouth never stops when it comes to the latest juicy gossip about everyone else around you. You've spun out of control and let your mouth run away from you. Maybe you struggle with compulsive lying. You don't know why, but nothing you ever say or no story you ever tell is the truth—it's always a little "embellished" to sound more interesting. Maybe you're the friend that's notorious for making promises you can't keep.

Whatever your struggle may be, you're letting those poor choices define who you are. You've bought into the lie that because this was a choice that you made one time, or how you've acted in the past, there's no way things could change for you. You have believed the lie that even if you tried, people wouldn't believe that you could change. Whatever it may be that you struggle with—if you've caved to living out a reputation that was dealt to you by a poor choice that you made in your past—you are letting the enemy win.

Girls, my heart breaks for you as I see countless young women believe the lies that the enemy has been feeding you—that you are used up, worthless, not good enough. There is a very real battle raging led by a very real enemy who is out to destroy our lives and to strip us of the life that Jesus died to give us.

1 Peter 5:8 paints a pretty serious warning for us: "Be serious! Be alert! Your adversary the Devil is prowling around like a roaring lion, looking for anyone he can devour" (HCSB).

He is a roaring lion looking for ANYONE he can devour...and his main goal is destroy our lives! You see, most girls after one bad choice, just give up and throw in the towel. They're done! Defeated. Ruined. But we just cannot give up that easily and cave to the idea that because of one bad decision THAT is what you have to then become!

Let me tell you today...it's time to RECLAIM that reputation! The time has come for you to move forward and stop looking behind. Today is the day to stop believing the lies from the enemy and fight for your reputation. This week, we're going to look at five new areas of "junk" that need to be stripped away and removed from our lives so that we can be successful at reclaiming reputation. A good reputation is a hard thing to get back. Typically, once it's gone, it takes a lifetime to get back! But girls, here is the good news that Jesus wants you to hear today: IT CAN AND NEEDS TO BE RECLAIMED!

It's going to be hard. It's going to take a ton of effort on your part. But most importantly, it's going to have to be JESUS in you. So, it's time to make an effort to move forward and reclaim what is yours—a redeemed, sanctified life given as a free gift to you through Jesus Christ and His death on the cross.

It's time to get up and fight!

JUNK: LYING

> Truthful lips endure forever, but a lying tongue lasts only a moment.
> **Proverbs 12:19** (HCSB)

> The LORD detests lying lips, but he delights in those who tell the truth.
> **Proverbs 12:22** (NLT)

Is lying ever okay?

Let's say your best friend asks for your opinion on her outfit—you know it's not flattering but you don't want to hurt her feelings. What do you say? Is it okay to lie in this situation? How about when you say you are sick just so you can stay home from school and work on the project you forgot to finish? Is that little white lie harmful? How about when a guy asks you out that you are not interested in—is making up a story about plans you don't really have, just to save his feelings, okay?

Most of us probably sleep like a baby at night even if we have lied multiple times throughout the day. We live in culture that excuses lies. We call them "little white lies" or "exaggerations" or "half truths," but in reality, anytime we lie, we sin. It's actually very simple—and very destructive.

Think about it. Lying can be the act of telling something that isn't true—like when you tell your friend that you are going to this place but really go somewhere else or when you tell your parents you did this but you really did something different. Here's the flip side, lying can also be about what you don't say—like when you leave out certain details so your parents won't get upset with you. After all, it seems harmless enough. And that is where the issue comes in. When you deem certain forms of lying as acceptable you are giving the devil a foothold into your life, and sin always escalates.

If you want to reclaim your reputation and your identity in Christ, then it is important to deal with the "junk" of lying. It's something that needs to be sanded away so that your reputation can be refinished and restored to all that the Lord designed it to be. One of the first steps to changing your habits is to begin agreeing with God about it. Read Proverbs 12:22 again. Notice how God feels about your lying— He DETESTS it. That, girlfriend, is a great place to start salvaging your identity.

DIY:

Re-Think (Journal & Pray):

+ Get Real: List the places, times, and people that you are most likely to "lie" about or to.
+ Write out a confession to the Lord about your lying tongue and confess that you've not been agreeing with Him about untruth.
+ Journal your thoughts about what it will take to reclaim your reputation so that people know that you mean what you say and can believe you.
+ Pray and ask the Lord to convict you BEFORE you lie or speak deceitfully. Ask that He make you very sensitive to the Holy Spirit—be sure to respond correctly when you feel conviction!

Re-Visit the Word:

+ Proverbs 12:19
+ Proverbs 12:22
+ Read these verses in various translations. Pick the one that speaks loudest to you and pray those words daily until you begin to see change occurring in your life.

Re-Claim:

In small group or with your accountability partner, discuss the truth of Proverbs 12:22—God either detests what you say or takes delight in you. Which would you rather be part of? Why? What else delights the Lord? Look the word "delight" up in an online Bible concordance and find some other verses about what makes God delight.

Discuss the other places you have not delighted the Lord and agree to hold each other accountable especially about the "lying tongue" issue. Give each other permission to call the other out when you hear talk that is not truthful—you may want to develop some code word or phrase to use so that just your group knows what's up.

JUNK: CHEATING

> Honesty guides good people; dishonesty destroys treacherous people.
> **Proverbs 11:3 (NLT)**

In today's society, it seems like every time we turn around there is another athlete, celebrity, or politician who is having a press conference where they're admitting that they've cheated. Whether it's adultery in their marriage, an athlete cheating to advance his career, or even as small as a student cheating on a test via text messaging, it's everywhere today.

In January 2013, world renowned cyclist and seven-time winner of the Tours de France Lance Armstrong confessed in an interview with Oprah Winfrey that after years of speculation he was in fact guilty of using performance enhancing drugs to advance his career. Armstrong was seen by many in the world to be an amazing athlete and role model, not only in the cycling world but also in the realm of the cancer charity, Livestrong Foundation, that he founded back in 1997 after his own personal battle with cancer. In that interview with Oprah, it only took a moment for years of a successful career to come crashing down, all because of an integrity issue. Now, given, this story about Lance Armstrong's career is a huge deal when it comes to cheating, but all cheating, character, and integrity issues begin somewhere.

Let's face it. If you cheat in the little things, you'll cheat in the big stuff in life too. So here is my challenge for you today: ask yourself what kind of girl do you really want to be someday? The decisions that you make today, even in the small things, will affect who you will become tomorrow. We always need to be striving for who we want to be in the future as we walk this journey of life.

Today's Scripture in Proverbs 11:3 reminds us that "honesty guides good people [and] dishonesty DESTROYS." Whether it's just cheating on homework or a decision some time in the future that will affect your marriage, don't cut corners. Dishonesty will always bring about destruction and nothing positive will ever come out of our own selfish gain. Most of us have cheated at some point in our lives. It may be small or big, but the reality is that there are consequences to the choices we make, and some decisions in life have some pretty painful consequences.

Whether it's to pay the corrected amount owed at a restaurant if the bill comes back with an error on it, come clean with your teacher about copying a paper in English class, or deciding ahead of time not to text the questions from your Pre-Algebra mid-term to your best friend, when you do the right thing in the little things you'll be able to do the right things in the bigger issues in life.

So, start with the little things. It may not seem like a big deal to you now, but when you make a commitment to yourself to live your life today to be the woman you hope to become tomorrow, I promise you'll make some choices differently. It's called character. And if you're a believer in Christ, God calls us all to a high standard when it comes to our character. Character is who are you when no one else is looking. You can't take shortcuts in life; you will never live a life of peace if you do. God doesn't call you to be the girl to say one thing and do another.

DIY:

Re-Think (Journal & Pray):

+ Write out your goals for what kind of woman that you want to be someday.
+ What are some things that may need to change in your life for you to achieve that goal to be the woman you described?

+ Write out in a journal or in the inside cover of your Bible the definition of character: "Who you are when no one else is looking."
+ Confess to the Lord the "little stuff" (or the "big stuff")where you have taken shortcuts in your life when it comes to honesty and your character.
+ Accept the Lord's forgiveness. Remember we're not defining ourselves regarding our past choices, but we're moving forward to find freedom in Christ (Gal. 5:1).

Re-Visit the Word:

+ Memorize: Proverbs 11:3

Re-Claim:

In small group or with your accountability partner, discuss some struggles in your life as it relates to cheating. (Honesty and trust are key when it comes to accountability.) What are ways you can be pro-active when tempted to cheat or take shortcuts in the future?

Make right any wrongs you need to take care of. If confession needs to take place with a teacher, a parent, or a friend, take action so you can move forward with how the Lord wants to continue to "salvage" your identity in Him.

Day Three

JUNK: BROKEN PROMISES

God's way is perfect. All the LORD's promises prove true. He is a shield for all who look to him for protection. **2 Samuel 22:31** (NLT)

You've probably heard about or seen the movie *The Vow*. What made it so popular? It's a great love story (based on a real life account) about a couple who end up together against all odds. After suffering from amnesia due to a car accident, the main character, Paige, can't remember her life before the wreck and has no memory of the love she shared with her husband Leo. Even so, Leo remains faithful to the vow he made to love her in sickness and in health. He refuses to give up on the relationship in spite of seemingly insurmountable obstacles. This kind of commitment speaks to us because keeping promises is highly unusual in our world today.

I'm definitely not holding this movie up as a good model for how to do relationships, but I do believe that the reason so many females are enthralled with it is because it demonstrates what can happen when people vow to do something and keep their commitment. That is such a foreign concept to most of us that we are fascinated by it.

Do you remember ever wanting something really badly and then when you found out that you were going to get it, you couldn't believe it? So what do you do? You ask the other person to "promise me" or you may "pinky promise." What's the point of these actions? It's all about trying to guarantee that the promise will not be broken. Have you ever wondered why gangs do such dangerous initiations for

40

people coming into their group? It's to try and put a guarantee on their loyalty because just their word isn't enough to make them feel safe and confident.

Why such extremes? Because people break promises. They do. You can probably immediately think of promises that have been broken in your life, whether by you or someone else. We live in a society that doesn't value the keeping of promises. On every level from the promise to be "best friends forever" in kindergarten to marriage vows, promises just don't carry the weight they used to or that they should.

The junk that you need to think about today is two-fold. On one side, how have you let your own trustworthiness slide since, after all, no one really takes promises seriously any more anyway? That's actually not true—your reputation depends on you being a person who keeps her word. Read Zechariah 8:16-17 (NIV): "'These are the things you are to do: Speak the truth to each other, and render true and sound judgment in your courts; do not plot evil against your neighbor, and do not love to swear falsely. I hate all this,' "declares the LORD."

Hmm...once again we find something that God can't stand. Fair warning, if you plan to truly reclaim your reputation, you have to be willing to do the hard things.

The second side of this issue is: How have you let the fact that people break promises affect the way you view God and His trustworthiness? One of the greatest things about our God is that He ALWAYS keeps His promises. The Lord is our perfect example of trustworthiness because we can count on Him to do every single thing He says He will do. Every. Single. One. Count on it.

DIY:

Re-Think (Journal & Pray):

+ What broken promises have strongly affected your life?
+ When you consider that God never breaks a promise, how does that change the way you feel about Him and increase your trust in Him?

+ What promise of God do you struggle to accept and believe?
+ Confess and repent of your own lack of faith in the Lord. Ask that He bring today's verses to mind as a challenge to stand by your word and to trust that He will ALWAYS stand by His.

Re-Visit the Word:

+ 1 Corinthians 1:9
+ When you feel tempted to doubt what God says about you or to you through His Word, remember this verse and quote it until you believe that you were called into fellowship with Him!

Re-Claim:

In small group or with your accountability partner, discuss the following questions: How do broken promises affect us? What can you do to in order to establish a different pattern for your own promises? When people break their promises to you, what should be your response?

As so many people in Scripture found out—King David, Joseph, Sarah and Abraham, etc.—sometimes when God promises something, fulfillment of that promise can take longer than we think to come about. How does waiting for God's promise to come challenge you?

HEALING BROKENNESS:

By the time you get to your teen/young adult years, you have probably already experienced a time when someone did not follow through with his or her promise to you. This can be very hurtful and can leave you in a position to vow or promise never to act like certain people, and it can also leave you with an inability to trust others. It is important to remember that everyone is flawed, and the only perfect person that ever walked the earth was Jesus. We can fully trust God because He always follows through with His Word. If you have experienced people letting you down and not following through, you may be left in a vulnerable position to make vows to yourself, creating unhealthy expectations of yourself and others.

Promises broken to you:
+ But he said he loved me.
+ My dad promised he would come.
+ I will not tell anyone; your secret is safe with me.
+ We will be best friends forever.

Broken promises can be very painful and can often leave you in a place lacking the ability to trust people. It is important to remember that all humans are flawed; they are not perfect. Just like someone may have broken a promise to you, at some point you could have broken a promise to her. Don't let one bad encounter or experience shape how you view the world, yourself, and others.

Think about vows you made as a child:
+ I will never be like my mother.
+ I will never be like my father.
+ I will never sing because someone said I was off key.
+ I will be rich when I grow up if it's the last thing I do.
+ I'm never getting married because marriages don't last.
+ I will never act like that towards my kids.

Unfortunately making vows like this can set us up for failure later in life because our words have so much power. Ask the Lord to reveal to you unwise vows that you have made and ask Him to be the one to break them in Jesus' name. Grieving the disappointment of someone not following through with her word can be a difficult process and may be something you need to go through with a counselor or someone you really trust. It is important to realize deeper hurts can affect how we view and treat others, and the Lord wants you set free from any unholy vows or any pain you may be carrying from broken promises.

JUNK: HYPOCRISY

> In the same way, on the outside you appear to people as righteous but on the inside you are full of hypocrisy and wickedness. **Matthew 23:28** (NIV)

In April 2013, the Barna Research Group did a study asking the question, "Are more Christians today like Jesus or like the Pharisees?" They asked questions to determine whether the actions and attitude of "Christians" when interacting with others were more like Jesus or more like the self-righteous attitudes and behaviors of the Pharisees of the New Testament. The results broke my heart, as this research uncovered that 51 percent of the people used for this study mirrored behaviors and attitudes more like the self-righteous and arrogant pharisaical ways. Only 14 percent of "self-identified Christians" (only 1 out of 7) seemed to represent the actions and attitudes consistent with those of Jesus.[3]

If you're reading this and thinking "The Pharisees...what is she talking about?" Here's a quick synopsis. The Pharisees were a self-righteous group of religious leaders in the Jewish temple during Jesus' earthly ministry that He encountered quite often throughout the Gospels. This is also the same group of men that didn't believe that Jesus Christ was the Messiah, the Son of God, and had Jesus arrested and crucified. In Matthew 23:28, Jesus addressed this group of men when He said, "In the same way, on the outside you seem righteous to people, but inside you are full of hypocrisy and lawlessness."

Jesus was disgusted by their religious rituals done to be seen by man, their judgmental, legalistic views, and their "holier than thou" way of living. They were blind to their own need for a Savior. They walked on this earth and talked face-to-face with Jesus, but they couldn't see past their religious law or themselves.

We live in a "Christian culture" where more than 75 percent of Americans claim to be a "Christian." We know that not all, but a whole lot of that 75 percent look like chameleons rather than looking anything like Jesus. They're one way when at church, they are a different people around their family, and they are totally different when around their friends at school. Girls, this lifestyle is the definition of a hypocrite!

Sadly, too many Christians today have lost their "religious identity" in compromising with the ways of the world. How heartbreaking it must be for our Heavenly Father to see His children using His free gift of grace, through Jesus, as a license to do whatever they want because they know that He ultimately loves and forgives. Trying to fit in and play the part of both worlds, the spirit and the flesh, will NEVER work, and it's not what Jesus Christ has called us to as a follower of Him.

The point of today's topic is not to leave you feeling beaten up, although I do hope that the Holy Spirit might just use this to bring about conviction in your life because let's be honest, we can all use conviction in our hearts and lives. This is where change can occur, transforming us to look a little more like Jesus.

So, once again, it's time that we rise up and live out the change that God has brought to our lives by the gift of grace through His Son, Jesus Christ! If you want to know more about how He lived, how He loved, how He would handle certain situations, and just how much He loves YOU, then it's time to get to know Him better! Dig into His Word, read about His life, and when you do, you will fall more in love with Him. In time you will start looking a whole lot more like Jesus and less like the Pharisees.

DIY:

Re-Think (Journal & Pray):

+ Would you say that you might fall in the 51 percent of the population who claim to be "Christian" but have the attitude and actions of a Pharisee?
+ What are some ways that you've compromised the gospel by living like a chameleon? Journal and confess these things to the Lord.
+ What are some changes that you need to make to challenge yourself to display a life that's more like Jesus and less like the world? Ask God to help give you the strength to live out a REAL and AUTHENTIC faith.

Re-Visit the Word:

+ Matthew 23:28
+ Matthew 15:7-9
+ Isaiah 29:13

Re-Claim:

In small group or with your accountability partner, discuss ways to keep each other accountable to live a life more like Jesus and less like the Pharisees. Look back together at the Gospels and discuss other encounters when Jesus addresses the hypocrisy of the Pharisees. Keep each other accountable so you won't fall into living like a "chameleon." Pray together against being a believer like the ones described in Matthew 15 and Isaiah 29.

JUNK: MANIPULATION

> This is what the LORD says your Redeemer, the Holy One of Israel: "I am the LORD your God, who teaches you what is best for you, who directs you in the way you should go." **Isaiah 48:17** (NIV)

Women are notorious for taking care of the details. When a prom group gets planned or a party needs details, who takes care of it? We do. That's part of how we were wired, but there is an issue that we as women face—the temptation to manipulate. The definition for manipulate is to handle or control a tool, mechanism, etc., typically in a skillful manner. It can also mean to alter, edit, or move text on a computer.

Does that sound like you? Before you say no, think about it a little more. How often are you tempted to involve yourself in some of the different "junk" we've been talking about this week in order to make something happen the way you think it should? Have you lied, cheated, broken a promise, or been hypocritical and justified it by telling yourself that it was for a good reason? You aren't the first to think like that, but please try to learn from other people's mistakes.

Remember the story of Abraham and Sarah? God told Abraham that he would be the father of many nations. But one problem. No kids. He and his wife Sarah were childless. So how in the world could he possibly be the father of many nations? Sarah got tired of waiting for the promise to be fulfilled (DANGER) and took matters into her own hands (see the definition of manipulate, to handle or control in a skillful manner). You see, Sarah looked at her own body, well into old age, and thought, "I'm not going to be part of what God promised." So she started manipulating the plan and she sent her servant, Hagar, to sleep with her own husband—there were no fertility clinics or other options. Then after the servant got pregnant, things got messy. Eventually Sarah did get pregnant in her nineties as part of God's plan, but because of her manipulation, there were issues to deal with that got rough. The son by the servant was named Ishmael, and when he came into the world, the stage was set for the birth of the Arab nation.[4] The son by Sarah was named Isaac and his descendants were the Israelite people. To this day there is strife (think fighting and wars) between these two groups of people.

Here's the lesson for us. When we refuse to let God work out details in our lives Himself, things get messy and we miss out on the peace we desperately desire.

A wise woman learns from those who have gone before her. When you feel yourself start to take over and manipulate things (especially if it means brining some "junk" into your life) stop and think about Sarah.

DIY:

Re-Think (Journal & Pray):

+ How often do you tend to manipulate things? Even if you have others' best interests at heart?
+ What or who offers you the greatest temptation to manipulate?
+ How can you make some changes to resist the temptation to manipulate?
+ What other negatives happen when you choose to manipulate?

Re-Visit the Word:

+ Genesis 16:1-18:14

Re-Claim:

In small group or with your accountability partner, discuss lessons you can learn from today's story. What does Sarah's manipulation reveal about her faith? Who does she blame for the fact that she didn't have a child already? What does she do when the news of her impending pregnancy comes? What was the great lesson learned? Talk about how to apply these thoughts and truths to your life.

3

Restore Realness

Therefore, with your minds ready for action, be serious and set your hope completely on the grace to be brought to you at the revelation of Jesus Christ. As obedient children, do not be conformed to the desires of your former ignorance. But as the One who called you is holy, you also are to be holy in all your conduct; for it is written, Be holy, because I am holy.
1 Peter 1:13-16 (HCSB)

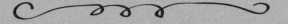

One of the coolest things to see when redoing old or beaten up furniture is when you get the junk all stripped away and the real beauty of the wood begins to show. It's exciting because then you get a vision of how the piece is supposed to look, seeing the natural lines of the wood.

I remember one of the first times I refinished something, and when I had gotten to this point in the process, my tendency was to try and sand away every little thing I could see. My friend, who knew much more about it than me, told me not to go crazy sanding. She said, "Those are some of the natural 'flaws' in the wood and instead of trying to sand them away in search of perfection, if you will accept them and finish the piece right, then it will actually be MORE beautiful because of the realness of the wood." She was completely right.

Sometimes in our search for perfection, we are tempted to lose our "realness." We feel like we have too many flaws for people to accept us the way we are so we pretend to be something we aren't in order to feel better about ourselves. This is a recipe for disaster and will set you up for identity crisis for sure. Please understand that being real and authentic is the only way to really live the abundant life that God has for you. AND get this, you are actually more beautiful, just like my furniture, when you allow God to use you and your imperfections. Let's face it girls, we all have imperfections so why not be real about them and let God do what only He can do with us?

This week we will discuss some of the "junk" that needs to be stripped away from our lives in order to truly salvage our identities. Each one is probably going to be tough for you to work through because you might be scared of what people will say if you begin to actually live a REAL,

AUTHENTIC life. Guess what? They have no power over you except what you give them. The world will always come after anyone who stands for Christ and tries to live His way—in holiness. What we need is FEWER mean girls who put others down to make themselves feel better and MORE sisterhood, people who accept each other the way we are and encourage each other to be real and authentic. Yes—I know that sounds a little like a Tyler Perry movie, but the truth is still there

When we live authentic lives, we win. We get the freedom to be ourselves, and our lives are a stronger testimony for who God is, which means we are better examples of Christ. I once was sharing with a lost person about Jesus. She wasn't ready to hear about Him. So we just got to know each other, and over time she finally accepted Christ. When asked later what was said that made her know she needed Jesus her reply was, "It was when I saw her be real and knew that her life wasn't perfect but she still had faith that I realized I needed her Savior myself." That's HUGE.

Authenticity is incredibly freeing, but more importantly, it can lead to evangelism—which is what we are called to do anyway! Those things in us that we think of as imperfections, God uses to make us unique. Instead of trying to hide them, let's allow God to refinish us the way He intends and use us for His glory. Come on, let your true self shine—join the sisterhood!

Day One

JUNK: ISOLATION

> While Moses held up his hand, Israel prevailed, but whenever he put his hand down, Amalek prevailed. When Moses' hands grew heavy, they took a stone and put it under him, and he sat down on it. Then Aaron and Hur supported his hands, one on one side and one on the other so that his hands remained steady until the sun went down. So Joshua defeated Amalek and his army with the sword. **Exodus 17:11-13** (HCSB)

Our society is loud. Noise and people constantly surround us, yet in the midst of the chaos of our lives it can sometimes be a lonely place. We smile, we nod, and we laugh with friends at the lunch table. But at the end of the day, is there a possibility that you feel isolated and alone? If so, why do you think this is?

Many of us surround ourselves with lots of people, but if we are honest, are we truly known by anyone? I'm talking about exposing not only the good, but the bad and ugly as well. As girls, we tend to isolate ourselves out of fear of being exposed by things that are hidden and buried in our lives. We view being open and transparent in friendships as being weak or vulnerable. And exposing what's really going on inside is simply out of the question.

Are you putting so much energy into the girl you're pretending to be, instead of addressing the REAL you? Maybe you're ashamed of some aspect of your life and have been dealing with it for years by isolating the person you truly are. Friendships these days require so much "maintenance," whether in appearance, social status, and "people-pleasing," we just get caught up in covering our flaws. However, it's in exposing these things in our lives that we take the first step toward overcoming them. We need true, deep, trustworthy friendships! It's in our vulnerable, exposed weaknesses that we can be freed.

In preparing to write this, because we love the message, Rachel and I chose the story in Exodus 17 about the battle against the Amalekites to illustrate this point. Moses, one of the strongest leaders in Scripture is at a desperate moment of weakness. He's leading a battle, with the help of the Lord, but he must keep his staff raised in the air in order for the Israelites to win. As time goes on and the battle continues, he becomes exhausted and can no longer keep the staff raised in the air so the Israelites begin to lose. But Moses has Aaron. Aaron comes along side him with a guy named Hur. They stand on either side of Moses and hold up his arms, keeping his staff lifted in the air! The Israelites win the battle with the help of the Lord, the leadership of Moses, and the huge support (literally) from Aaron and Hur.

Please don't miss the point of why we are using this story to demonstrate isolation. It's not about the battle. It is about the vulnerability of one man and his need for support in a moment of exhaustion. God gave them the victory through a collective effort of His people supporting one another through life's battles. We were never meant to fight alone or live in isolation.

It's SO vital for us as girls to surround ourselves with other trustworthy believers, someone we can have "real talk" with. This person or people should be mature in their faith, willing to listen, and empathize with you without judgment. At the same time, they should challenge you to continue pursuing and loving Jesus.

Like Moses, we all need people like Aaron and Hur in our lives. So, begin TODAY being that type of friend you are praying for and you are hoping to find. We need to be asking God for deep, meaningful relationships with people who will come alongside us in our moments of weakness and hold our arms up!

DIY:

Re-Think (Journal & Pray):

+ Examine your heart and your life. Ask yourself if there are things keeping you "isolated." Seek God first and foremost with these issues of isolation and prepare your heart for today's Re-Claim section.
+ Ask the Lord to bring someone into your life who can be your "Aaron." If you already have someone in your life like this, thank the Lord again for that relationship! Take some time to reflect on how you're doing in that relationship. Are YOU returning the favor and holding up the arms of others who need it?
+ If you do not have someone like this in your life, begin praying and asking the Lord to bring a relationship like Moses and Aaron into your life.
+ Take a minute to show those in your life who are challenging you or who have helped you stand up during tough times how grateful you are for them! Write a note. Send a thankful text.

Re-Visit the Word:

+ Exodus 17:8-16
+ Philippians 2:4

Re-Claim:

In small group or with your accountability partner, discuss ways you've isolated your "TRUE self." Whether it's pretending or putting up a front out of fear of feeling "exposed" emotionally, talk about why we tend to avoid dealing with reality by isolating ourselves.

If there are some issues that you need to bring up with your small group leader or spiritual mentor, it's time to talk. Freedom comes when things are brought into the light and dealt with in community.

This is a safe place. There's no judgment during this time and what is voiced during this session STAYS HERE! Whatever you do, don't isolate yourself from those who can point you to truth as you heal. Stay connected and let God show His love through those around you!

HEALING BROKENNESS:

There is definitely a difference between isolation, loneliness, and being alone. It is important to realize that some people are introverts, and they need time to be alone in order to recharge, refuel, and be ready to conquer their day! However it is also important to know we are social beings, created to be in relationship with one another and interdependent on each other for survival! God is an integral part of healthy relationships with others. If we are looking for others to fill a space in our hearts that only God is meant to fill, we will never be satisfied in our relationships.

Ask yourself the following questions:
+ Do I have someone to turn to when I have a tough day?
+ In a crisis, can I name at least 2 people that I know I can turn to?
+ Am I trying to fill my need for social interaction through social media?
+ When I am alone, am I constantly thinking of how I'd like to be around other people?
+ Am I trying to get people to fill a God-shaped hole?

To take this even further, it is so important as young women that we have people who can speak into our lives. Someone that is older, or at least more mature in her faith, is a great start. On this journey of restoration, it helps to have people in our lives who display characteristics we are longing for—role models, leaders, and mentors!

In addition, we do not only have to worry about ourselves, but Scripture tells us in James 5:19-20 to go after any brother or sister who wanders off. It is so easy in difficult times to think that you are the only one who has ever felt this way or has ever experienced what you are going through, but remember, you are not alone. If you feel you are isolated, ask yourself if there are things you can do to change your circumstance. For example, maybe you can call a friend, get involved in a club at your school or in your community, pick up a hobby, take an extra class doing something you love, serve and volunteer at church, plan a get together with close friends, or get plugged in to activities that involve others. When you start focusing on helping others, it will really help you to not wallow in your own sorrow!

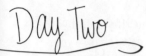

JUNK: CONFLICT

> Therefore, if you are offering your gift at the altar and there remember that your brother or sister has something against you, leave your gift there in front of the altar. First go and be reconciled to them; then come and offer your gift.
> **Matthew 5:23-24 (NIV)**

I hate conflict. Really hate it. I love when everyone gets along and no one is upset or mad or whatever. The problem is that when you have people around, you will have conflict, or as we like to call it in girl world—"drama." Even if it's not something you seek out. Whether you're like me and avoid conflict or you're the one who wants to stir things up—this day is for you.

It's virtually impossible to avoid all drama. So, what we have to do is learn how to deal with it in a way that honors God. After all, when you read Matthew 5:23-24 you can see that He is pretty serious about how we relate to other people. Look at it again, the Word says if you start to give an offering and remember that someone has something against you (conflict) then you're supposed to go and get right with her and THEN come back and give your offering. Wow. How many of us really do that? I mean seriously, who of us takes settling conflict to that level? Not many.

Think about it. Why don't we work out conflict more readily? Probably because resolving it requires humbling ourselves, and who likes to do that? But here's the deal, when we cherish relationships and work through conflict, we experience a sense of peace. Yes—PEACE. Galatians 5 lists the fruit of the Spirit and look what's included— love, joy, PEACE, etc. Guess what that means? We are to bring peace to situations and embrace peace even in the midst of relational struggles. When you constantly involve yourself in conflict then you aren't displaying the fruit of the Spirit like you need to. That explains a lot doesn't it?

When the fruit of the Spirit isn't being produced in your life then nothing else will be quite right. You will be reaping the wrong kinds of things and probably feeling lots of frustration and dissatisfaction, which in turn can fuel the temptation for you to engage in different kinds of conflict. As you work toward "realness" and authenticity this week, deal with drama and conflict in a way that makes a real difference in your quest to restore your identity.

In DIY you can find some specific steps that will help if you feel like the victim of unprovoked conflict. It will also be helpful if you've realized that YOU are most often the source of conflict. Both sides of this week's "junk" need to be dealt with in order to become the treasure you were intended to be.

DIY:

Re-Think (Journal & Pray):

+ Be honest. Do you start conflict and drama? Why?
+ What is the danger for you if you don't resist the temptation to get into conflict all the time?
+ When have you felt like a victim of drama or conflict? How does that affect the way you see yourself or tempt you to become less "real"?
+ What do you see as the relationship between lack of authenticity and conflict?
+ Write out a prayer confessing and repenting your involvement in conflict.
+ Do what Matthew 5:23-24 says and make things right between you and anyone you are in conflict with.

Re-Visit the Word:

+ Matthew 18:23-35
+ One of the biggest issues in conflict resolution is forgiveness. God said to forgive because He forgave you.

Re-Claim:

In small group or with your accountability partner, discuss the following questions: Why is forgiveness so hard when it comes to peers who have mistreated you? How can remembering that you have been forgiven of a whole lot make it easier to forgive when you need to? When you're tempted to jump into conflict or drama, what can you do to stop it before it starts?

Pray and ask the Lord to make you super sensitive to His Spirit and invite Him to convict you even before you contribute to conflict.

Day Three

JUNK: GOSSIP

Avoid godless chatter, because those who indulge in it will become more and more ungodly. **2 Timothy 2:16 (NIV)**

We've all had those moments when we're with some friends and a conversation begins that we know we shouldn't be a part of—you have that "check in your spirit" and you know that what you are hearing or even what you may be saying to someone else isn't okay. You know what I'm talking about...how many times have you talked behind someone's back or told your best friend's secret that she told to you in confidence? Maybe you feel as if it's your job to know everyone else's business, going to great lengths to "get the scoop" on what's going on in people's lives, even at the betrayal of other friends' trust.

Let's be real...our words can cause such hurt and they can deeply wound people! Gossip is a HUGE issue that plagues ALL of us as girls (even as "grown-up girls"). But the scary part is that for most women, this issue is as common in our daily lives as breathing! We so often forget the harm that can be done by our mouths, and it breaks my heart more than anything to think about how much power our mouths have, and yet, how lightly we handle its power.

I don't know about you, but as I read today's verse, 2 Timothy 2:16, it was like an "aha" moment for me. Here, Paul is giving us a strong command as believers to "AVOID godless chatter, because those who indulge in it will become more and more ungodly." The word "avoid" here means to shun, turn around, or turn your back on. And "godless chatter" in this passage is referring to empty, purposeless talk that fails to honor the Lord. That's pretty straightforward to me!

As we're on this journey of desiring change in our lives and wanting God to salvage our identity in Him, this issue is SO black and white. Yet we have made it gray. We especially tend to mask issues of gossip in the church with issues of concern for a friend, prayer requests of "Oh girl, we need to pray for _____, she's really struggling..." You get the picture. However, if we continue to let this issue of gossip go unaddressed in our lives, 2 Timothy gives the warning that those who indulge in it will become more and more ungodly. This is the complete opposite direction from where our Heavenly Father wants to see us moving. If we are supposed to be growing in our faith and looking more and more like Christ, gossip is an issue of junk that has GOT to be "stripped away" in order for us to live the life and have the pure heart that God desires for us to possess.

There is nothing more toxic, more devastating, or more destructive than gossip. We're all guilty of this issue, and we so desperately need to address it in our lives and bring it before the Father in an attitude of confession. Because until we deal with this junk, we'll continue to struggle on this journey of letting God salvage our identity in Him.

DIY:

Re-Think (Journal & Pray):

+ Take some time to humbly go before the Lord and confess any areas of gossip in your own life.
+ Be specific in bringing before the Lord times in your life that you have been guilty of gossip, whether it's doing the talking and/or listening without standing up to end the conversation.
+ Ask Him to give you the strength to stop gossiping and to turn your back on purposeless talk that fails to honor God. You can't argue with that!

Re-Visit the Word:

+ Memorize: 2 Timothy 2:16
+ Proverbs 20:19

Re-Claim:

In small group or with your accountability partner, discuss the following questions: How would you define gossip? Chatterers and godless chatter—did you catch both of those words from today's verses? How does gossip break trust in a relationship? Do you find that you need someone to hold you accountable in the area of gossip? What are some ways you can keep each other accountable when it comes to the issue of gossip in your life and within your friendships? Is there anyone you need to apologize to for the pain your careless words of gossip caused?

Day Four

JUNK: SOCIAL MEDIA ATTACKS

> Do everything without grumbling and arguing, so that you may be blameless and pure, children of God who are faultless in a crooked and perverted generation, among whom you shine like stars in the world. Hold firmly to the message of life. Then I can boast in the day of Christ that I didn't run or labor for nothing. **Philippians 2:14-16** (HCSB)

A friend of mine told me about how this past year has been so hard for her family because her daughter has been cyberbullied. She then went on to fill me in about how awful these other people had been to her 12 year-old. Although I have definitely heard about the issue and seen evidence of it firsthand through people at our church, this story was just heartbreaking for me. One morning as my friend went in to wake her daughter, she happened to look down and see an incoming text message response to her daughter's admission that she just couldn't take it any more and was thinking about killing herself.

That'll shock you as a parent and hopefully as anyone else. Imagine your friend, sister, coworker, or teammate taking her life because of being bullied by her peers. How would you feel? This issue of bullying is not new, but since the advent of cell phones and Internet access, it is much more intense because the victim can't ever escape. It isn't just occurring when they are around each other; the mean people keep on attacking at all hours.

I never cease to be amazed at what people, even ones who say they are Christians, will text or tweet that they wouldn't likely say in person. We MUST realize that our texts and tweets and Instagrams and Vines are all

64

another form of our voice—except that they are out there and recorded for all time. There are a lot of questions that come up with the junk of social media attacks, but today we address the "why" and "what" to do about them.

Bullying and attacking people through social media is usually based in a person's own insecurities. These are the people who only feel good about themselves if they can put others down. If this is you (think about how you typically treat others, do you trash talk them, criticize, or even subtweet them?) then your identity has definitely been stolen and is being used by the enemy. Read Philippians 2:14-16 again. It says to do everything without arguing, and if you don't, then you aren't living as a child of God should. Be sure you honestly walk through the DIY today so you can stop being used by the enemy!

What do you do if your identity is taking a hit from being bullied and put down through social media? As much as it is possible, protect yourself. My friend did everything from blocking text messages to changing cell phone numbers, but for some reason, these kids were so aggressive they found other apps that could get them around the blocks and back into attack mode. That's evil. There is no reason why you have to give evil an ear. You don't have to listen to or give your attention to those who are out to do the work of Satan. Fill your mind with the Truth from God's Word. Read what HE says about you; believe TRUTH, not the lies.

The key is that you refuse to listen to what others (who don't have a clue) say about you and find people who will support and encourage you in TRUTH. And don't miss the good news—when you learn to "do everything without grumbling and arguing" you will become "blameless and pure children of God" who "shine like stars in the universe" and all of that in the middle of a world that is crooked and depraved! Talk about an identity salvage...

DIY:

Re-Think (Journal and Pray):

+ If you're one who's been using social media to attack then stop! And confess it immediately. Pray and ask for forgiveness, then go to that person and ask forgiveness.

+ Ask God to reveal to you why you only feel good about yourself when you put someone else down. This study is for you because you MUST understand that you have worth as a child of God because of who you are in HIM. You will never live with a "salvaged" identity as long as this misguided thinking is part of your life.
+ Are you struggling with feelings of worthlessness because of how others have put you down?
+ Write out a prayer to the Lord asking Him to give you wisdom and discernment to believe His Truth over the lies of the enemy. Ask Him for strength to live in the Truth from here on out. Commit to ignore, delete, and avoid those who seek to tear you down. Take whatever steps you can to protect yourself and make sure someone else (parent, teacher, church leader, etc.) knows what is happening to you.

Re-Visit the Word:

+ 1 Peter 4:8
+ Philippians 2:14-16

Re-Claim:

In small group or with your accountability partner, discuss the following questions: When have you been involved in something that could be considered a social media attack? What was your motivation for those attacks? Why do you think so many people feel better about themselves when they put others down? What does the Bible have to say about treating your peers? How can you be better at believing the Truth of God's Word over the lies of the enemy?

JUNK: PEER PRESSURE

> The righteous choose their friends carefully, but the way of the wicked leads them astray. **Proverbs 12:26 (NIV)**

"You become like the people you hang out with." I heard this statement from my parents over and over again while I was growing up. I would always roll my eyes and think, "Yeah, yeah, whatever..." However, this simple yet strong statement was always looming in the back of mind as I walked through my teenage and young adult years. Your group of peers (the people you surround yourself with) are most likely the ones who will put pressure on you to conform to their ways of thinking or their ways of doing things.

Have you ever even given any thought to the people that you hang out with and how they influence the type of girl you are? You're more likely to compromise who you are at the hands of peer pressure if you're surrounding yourselves with godless friends, especially while living in this destructive, godless culture. Negative peer pressure happens when you're desperate to fit in or impress someone in order to be accepted, especially when you're willing to do whatever it takes to gain that acceptance. When you try to fit into a negative group, you're usually willing to compromise who you are and what you believe at any cost and all for people who will only pull you down. And can I just say...this never ends well. These moments of compromise, at the cost of the desire of acceptance, are almost always followed by heartache, lots of regret, and some pretty rough consequences. Negative people will influence you negatively. Bottom line.

On the flip side, there is a kind of peer pressure that can be positive in our lives. If "you become like the people you hang out with," then when you surround yourself with godly people, it will leave a godly impact on your life. Those people who make you want to strive to be a better person...who hold you to a higher standard...who lift you up instead of tearing you down...these are the people that point you more towards Jesus than those who lead you away from Him. When you surround yourself with a group of friends that are like-minded in conviction, your relationships will be more secure and the desire to impress by doing destructive things that compromise who you are is a little more obsolete. However, so often in ministry, I see those students who begin with a positive influence in their lives but then they start hanging out with a group of their peers in order to "be a good influence" or pull someone up from the lifestyle they're in, only to find themselves being pulled right down with them. It's a lot more difficult to pull someone up than it is to be pulled down. So be careful!

Let's take a look at God's Word when it comes to friends and their influence on our lives. There are so many verses in God's Word that address healthy friendship. Let's look at Proverbs 12:26, "The righteous choose their friends carefully, but the way of the wicked leads them astray."

Pretty self-explanatory if you ask me! So, let me ask you today, do you choose your friends carefully?

Peer pressure will always be present in our lives. Remember in Chapter 2 when we talked about our very real enemy that is out to destroy our lives? He wants to trip us up and see us led astray from the way of righteousness with Christ. You have the power to choose your friends carefully, and it's time to quit compromising your convictions all for the approval of a crowd that will only lead you down the path of destruction. It's time to stand up to peer pressure and choose those who you're going to allow to influence you!

DIY:

+ Spend time today journaling and praying to the Lord, if there are issues that need to be confessed and resolved before Him, take time to do so.
+ Has there been a time in your life when you've compromised your beliefs all in order to fit in? How did that work out for you?

Re-Visit the Word:

+ Romans 12:2
+ 1 Corinthians 10:13
+ 1 John 2:15-17

Re-Claim:

In small group or with your accountability partner, discuss the following questions: What are some areas of negative peer pressure in your life? What are some positive areas of peer pressure?

Let's go a little deeper into the Word of God. Discuss the passages from today's "Re-Visit the Word." What do they say about you and how you are to handle this issue of peer pressure in your life? What so they say about God? Who are some people you need to choose to surround yourself with in order to have godly peer pressure? Are there others who you need to let go of that affect you negatively?

4

PROJECT:

Repossess Self-control

Watch and pray so that you will not fall into temptation.
The spirit is willing, but the flesh is weak.
Matthew 26:41 (NIV)

Whether you realize it or not, you are presented each day with two options. Are YOU going to be in control of the events and circumstances of your day, or, as a believer, are you going to allow the Holy Spirit to take control?

You see, it is like getting into a car every day. You can take control of the steering wheel and drive, not knowing what kind of "hazards," "traffic," or circumstances are coming your way, or you can hand over control to the Holy Spirit and let Him drive you through the events that you will face, acknowledging to the Lord that you have no clue what lies ahead of you that day. However, the Spirit knows full well what you will face, and He will give you all you need as you encounter each moment.

Choosing the Spirit to control our lives is a DAILY practice of surrender. We have to humble ourselves and ask the Lord for His help. We cannot, nor do we want to, walk the path of life on our own. But let's be realistic, even if we start off our day on the right foot, as the events of each day unfold we're quick to yank that "steering wheel" right of the hands of the Holy Spirit in our desperate attempt for control. And all too often we majorly mess things up. This is the daily struggle for every believer—the battle of the flesh vs. the spirit.

In Matthew 26:41, Jesus is talking to His disciples and addresses this struggle for them. It's still a battle for us as believers every day when we climb out of bed..."Watch and pray so that you will not fall into temptation. The spirit is willing, but the flesh is weak."

The Holy Spirit is ready and willing to lead, guide, and direct our path each day. But so often we don't even tap into the power, wisdom, peace, and self-control that the Spirit can provide in our lives. When we don't allow the Spirit to control us, "handing over our steering wheel," we're choosing to walk in our flesh, which is SO weak. As we choose to walk in our flesh we are choosing to call the shots, answer all the questions, and respond to the circumstances on our own, THINKING that we know better than God! And this is where things get so messy.

One especially difficult fruit of the Spirit from Galatians 5 is self-control. Self-control is not practiced often in our world today. In fact, we live in an "instant gratification," "do-whatever-feels-good" entitled society where people are impulsive with little concern for the consequences of their actions—this is the opposite of self-control. In addition to what Jesus says to us in Matthew 26, you can read more of what the Word says about the flesh vs. the spirit in Galatians 5:16-26.

So why do we need to "repossess" self-control? Because we need to NOT be in control but to let the Holy Spirit guide our every thought, word, and action.

This week we're going to tackle some pretty heavy topics that desperately need to be addressed. So buckle up and get ready for this ride we're about to take. As we begin this week of repossessing self-control, ask yourself: who is driving me?

JUNK: SELF-HARM AND ADDICTIONS

> Don't you know that your body is a sanctuary of the Holy Spirit who is in you, whom you have from God? You are not your own, for you were bought at a price. Therefore glorify God in your body. **1 Corinthians 6:19-20** (HCSB)

She felt like everything was out of her control. Her relationships, school, work—nothing felt right. Every time she looked in the mirror, she hated what she saw. It caused her disappointment, and she felt desperate to do something. Anything that would give her some control back or help her escape in some way...

Sadly the above description could be of many girls and young women today. According to the National Association of Anorexia Nervosa and Associated Disorders, 95 percent of those who have eating disorders are between the ages of 12 and 26. Around 25 percent of female college students deal with eating disorders.[5] Just as alarming, other forms of self harm such as cutting are also a growing issue among young females.

It's very likely that you or someone you know well has struggled with some of these issues and feelings. One high schooler who was seriously dealing with anorexia shared that it was all about her need to feel in control of something and her extreme dissatisfaction with her appearance. This girl is a Christian and had heard all the right stuff, but that didn't exempt her from having to face the struggle every day and choose which voices to listen to. You have the same choices: you can choose to listen to the world and try to take control of your life OR you can listen to the TRUTH that reminds you of what God says—you don't need to be MORE in control, you need to SURRENDER control to the Holy Spirit.

One of the greatest lies you hear is that these addictions and disorders are okay if they make you feel better because "it's your body and won't hurt anyone else." The problem is it isn't your body. If you read 1 Corinthians 6:19-20 you see a great word to cling to: "you are not your own...you've been bought at a price." That "price" is the blood of Jesus and means that whatever you do to your body matters to Him. And it's not just that you were bought with a price, but your body has an intended purpose—it is the temple of the Holy Spirit! Whatever you do to your body, how you think about it, treat it, or mistreat it matters because it is a sacred place where the Spirit of the living God resides. God has always been serious about the place where He dwells and He has chosen to dwell in us. That's a BIG deal...

DIY:

Re-Think (Journal & Pray):

+ What areas have you been guilty of abusing your body in some way?
+ Why do you give in to the temptation? What lies do you listen to that encourage you to mistreat your temple?
+ Confess the wrong thinking you have been engaging in and ask the Lord to forgive you and to give you wisdom to only believe Truth.

Re-Visit the Word:

+ 1 Corinthians 3:16-17

Re-Claim:

In small group or with your accountability partner, discuss the following: What does it mean to "glorify God with your body," as you think about taking care of yourself physically? What are you doing that is harmful to your body right now that you need to stop doing? How can you know if a bad habit or practice such as binge eating, dieting, extreme exercise, or whatever is becoming an addiction? When you are tempted to do something like we've talked about today to get some control over your life, how can remembering the words of 1 Corinthians 6:19-20 help?

HEALING BROKENNESS:

Self-harm tends to happen when someone's negative emotional tank feels like it is going to explode, and the very act of hurting one's self acts as a release to the intense overwhelming emotions she might be feeling. It is known as a coping mechanism; however, these are very harmful. If you or someone you know is using self-harm as a way to ease emotional pain, it is time to reach out for help! This could be a symptom of a deeper underlying issue that can definitely be treated. Bottom line, you are not alone, lots of people struggle with extreme emotions, especially during the teen years. However, hurting yourself is not the answer! The teen years can be very difficult, as there is an array of emotions you can feel in one day due to hormone changes, mood swings, and emotional imbalance. Some of this is very normal; however, using unhealthy methods to ease these changes is not and can even be life threatening!

As you go throughout your day, ask yourself what makes you happy and what eases your emotional tension? Add more of these things into your life. Find out what triggers your emotional swings, and attempt to solve problems in a new way. There are books, resources, and counselors who are willing to help and are just a phone call away!

Consider the following positive coping strategies:
+ Reduce the amount of stress in your life.
+ Reach out to friends and family and talk about what is bothering you.
+ Confront your problems rather than bottle them up inside.
+ Engage in activities that make you happy, i.e.: sports, art, music, reading, movies, etc.
+ Journal your feelings.

Most of all, remember it is not a coincidence you are reading this book, God wants you to experience freedom in Him and wants you to know that you are not alone in your struggle. He has a way out, and sometimes reaching a hand up to Him and asking Him for help is the best step you can take.

JUNK: SEXY INFLUENCES

> Do not let any part of your body become an instrument of evil to serve sin. Instead, give yourselves completely to God, for you were dead, but now you have new life. So use your whole body as an instrument to do what is right for the glory of God. **Romans 6:13** (NLT)

We all know that we live in an instant gratification, selfish, and twisted culture. Whether it's sexy images on a billboard or magazine cover, inappropriate pictures sent via text message, fantasy driven literature and romance novels, or inappropriate movies...girls today are overwhelmed with issues of sexuality in our culture. We titled today's junk as "sexy influences" because we want to make you aware of some issues that are influencing you negatively on a daily basis when it comes to sexuality. It's so important to recognize here who the real problem is in our culture. Just like the "forbidden fruit" in the Garden of Eden with Eve in Genesis 3, Satan is still up to no good when it comes to this department of deception. He wants nothing more than to take something that God intended for good and make it shameful; all the while, he takes something that is wrong according to the Word of God and makes it look delightful and fulfilling!

Today's topic may be perceived by some to be "taboo," but it's SO incredibly important to look into the truth found in God's Word and discover what He says about how to handle these issues! Notice in Romans 6:13 that it commands us, "DO NOT let ANY part of your body become an instrument of evil to serve sin." Your "body" includes all of you: body, mind, and spirit. So many young girls today think of purity only as an issue of waiting until marriage to have sex, but this is a huge misconception. Purity begins first in the battleground of our minds and also in our hearts. So take a moment and ask yourself: what am I putting into my mind and allowing to influence me? From love scenes in movies that you watch on the big screen to what you're looking at on the internet, or even what you're looking at in text message sent from a guy, does it honor the Lord?

Have you ever noticed how certain things you see (pictures, scenes from a movie, images on the Internet) are hard to erase out of your mind? That's because your mind is like a vault and what is put into it is locked there and sealed tight! Our minds are a powerful thing, especially when it comes to images but not just visual images. Let's also take a look at written literature.

There is a huge craze out there for women, young and old, to dive into "erotica reading." Erotica reading, simply put, is another version of pornography. While pornography uses visual images, erotica reading stimulates the body emotionally and sexually. This is any book that you would read where you'd find yourself awakening inappropriate sexual feelings, desires, and thoughts that take your mind into a fantasy world. Most young women who indulge in this kind of reading don't even realize the long-term effects that this emotional response creates. Partaking in this kind of reading, although it may seem simple and harmless, is a huge gateway into destructive and potentially long-term addictive behaviors that the Word of God tells us over and over again to avoid. These behaviors and thoughts can lead you on a path of exciting "highs" that are destructive and that will never satisfy—always leaving you longing for more or something new.

James 1:14-15 describes this progressive path that stems from temptation, "Temptation comes from our own desires, which entice us and drag us away. These desires give birth to sinful actions. And when sin is allowed to grow, it gives birth to death" (NLT). Notice that it states that when sin is allowed to grow, it gives birth to DEATH.

The truth is God created us as women for the sole purpose to bring Him glory! If what we're putting into our minds and things we're doing with our bodies do not honor Him, then we're missing our purpose in this life. The rest of Romans 6:13 goes on to say,

"Instead, give yourselves completely to God, for you were dead, but now you have new life. So use your whole body as an instrument to do what is right for the glory of God." If you're a follower of Jesus Christ, you have been given new life and you are to use your body (body, soul, and mind) as an instrument to do what is right for the glory of God.

DIY:

Re-Think (Journal & Pray):

+ Confess to the Lord any areas the Holy Spirit reveals to you about ways you've been deceived and have allowed things of our culture to seep in and influence your mind? Maybe it's movies, social media uploads, or texting—or maybe it's what you've been reading. Maybe it's something we didn't even mention today. Whatever it is, take some time to deal with it before the Lord.
+ Think of other areas of your life where you've allowed "sexy influences" from our culture to creep in undetected.
+ Ask the Lord for freedom and healing in areas where the innocence of your mind has been stripped away by our bold and twisted culture.

Re-Visit the Word:

+ Memorize: Romans 6:13
+ James 1:14-15
+ Philippians 4:8

Re-Claim:

In small group or with your accountability partner, discuss the following: What are some ways we justify movies we watch or books we read? Do they really have an affect on our minds? What are ways we can protect all of our "body" (Rom. 6:13) from other "sexy influences" of our culture? Is this issue really a big deal to you? Why or why not? How might these influences affect your life in the future?

JUNK: YOUR LOOK

> Your beauty should not come from outward adornment, such as braided hair and the wearing of gold jewelry and fine clothes. Rather, it should be that of your inner self, the unfading beauty of a gentle and quiet spirit, which is of great worth in God's sight. **1 Peter 3:3-4 (NIV)**

A few years ago I got up a little late and rushed out of the house to go work out. As I was pedaling away in a spin class patting myself on the back and thinking about how hard I was working and how many good results I would surely be seeing soon, the Holy Spirit asked me a question. I sensed Him speaking to my heart saying, "It's great that you are taking care of your body BUT what about your spirit?" Ouch. Then some verses I had memorized a while back worked their way into my head.

Check this out, 1 Timothy 4:7-8 says: "Have nothing to do with godless myths and old wives' tales; rather, train yourself to be godly. For physical training is of some value, but godliness has value for all things, holding promise for both the present life and the life to come" (NIV). Now, I sat there in complete conviction, not just about that morning, but about the number of times I had put my physical appearance and outward "look" ahead of my spiritual development and time with the Lord.

What would happen if we started focusing as much or more on how we look on the inside as we do on how we look on the outside? Good question. How long does it take you to get ready in the morning?

How much of that time is spent on how you look, outfit, hair, and makeup as compared to how much time is spent preparing yourself spiritually for the day? Of course, there is nothing wrong with wanting to present a pleasing appearance to the rest of the world, but the problem is when that becomes our main focus and what we put all of our time and energy into.

Over 50 billion dollars are spent on cosmetics in America each year. Wow. What could we do with some of that money redirected to the cause of Christ and reaching people with the gospel? How about you personally? Is your day made or ruined by how you think you look? Is a good day a good hair day or a clear complexion day? The sad thing is that most of us are holding ourselves up to an unrealistic model of what looks good anyway, so there is little to no hope of achieving what we aspire to.

I love those pictures you can see on magazines covers of the celebrities without their makeup and hair stylists. Why? Because it is such a good reminder that they are just regular people who have the same kind of issues as the rest of us when we look in the mirror. Scripture tells us that our beauty should be from the inside "that of your inner self, the unfading beauty of a gentle and quiet spirit, which is of great worth in God's sight."

None of us, celebrities included, can ever be perfect enough on the world's scale, but the inner beauty is another story. Those are things that you can do something about. Your outward beauty can be here today and gone tomorrow. Think about what a relief it could actually be in your life to develop godly characteristics that will never fade or be taken away by time or gravity. To be beautiful because of who you are and not how you look...

Letting the world define your look is junk that needs to be scraped away so your true beauty can shine through!

DIY:

Re-Think (Journal & Pray):

+ Evaluate the time you spend on physical appearance as compared to time you spend on spiritual development. Where is your focus?

- Confess and repent of any imbalances you see in your daily habits.
- Ask the Lord to convict you of those times when you are placing too much emphasis on your "look" and not enough on your inner beauty.
- Make a list of things you notice in other people that you consider beautiful; then make a list of the characteristics you want to display in your life. Be intentional about making them part of your daily life.

Re-Visit the Word:

- 1 Timothy 4:7-8
- Write this on your bathroom mirror or on a card that you see daily. Use it as a reminder to keep your priorities in line with God's Word.

Re-Claim:

In small group or with your accountability partner, discuss the following: Why do you hyper-focus on your physical appearance? What is unappealing about a girl/woman who is too concerned with her physical appearance? How can someone who is all about her "look" be a negative influence for the gospel? How can realigning your focus actually help you be more beautiful to others? What can you do to help each other keep a proper perspective on your appearance?

Day Four

JUNK: PREMARITAL SEX

> God's will is for you to be holy, so stay away from all sexual sin. Then each of you will control his own body and live in holiness and honor—not in lustful passion like the pagans who do not know God and his ways.
> **1 Thessalonians 4:3-5 (NLT)**

In this day and age, students are engaging in sexual relations as early as 11-12 years-old. Whether it is pornography, erotica novels, oral sex, homosexuality/bi-sexuality, or sexual intercourse, all are a highway to destruction and brokenness. Statistics say that 7 out of every 10 students have had sex by the age of 19 years old.[6] We know that temptation and issues of sexuality are around us 24/7! We live in a culture where "sex sells." You can hardly turn on the television without seeing a commercial that has sexuality written all over it. And what I really don't get is that they're using sex to try and sell us cars and even hamburgers! I mean, seriously?!

Girls, hear me when I say that sex is an amazing gift from God! It is not this dirty, shameful, harmful thing because God created it. The culturally "good girl" or the "church-going girl" has been told her whole life "NO-NO-NO!" when it comes to the issue of sex. After years of hearing no-no-no, without hearing the why, it gives us a skewed view of this gift God created. You see, if done in the context of marriage, which is what He created this gift of sex for, God says "YES-YES-YES!" That's where we've gone wrong in our society today. Our culture has cheapened this amazing gift God designed and messed things all up!

Here is something that I found to be really cool. The Hebrew word for "sex" is *yada*, which is kind of comical to me because I immediately think of "yada, yada, yada," like what you're thinking when you are bored listening to someone and all you're hearing is "blah, blah, blah"...but this if far from what this Hebrew word for sex means.

Get ready for this...*yada* literally means to know or to be known; to be deeply respected, mentally, emotionally, and physically. I don't know about you, but that sure isn't how I've heard the world define sex today!

God gave us this amazing and precious gift within the boundaries of marriage as a form of intimacy between a husband and his wife to know each other in a way that no one else does. Like we talked about a little in Day 2 of this week, Satan has taken this amazing gift of sex that God created and has cheapened it, twisted it, and made it seem okay to partake of with no strings attached. But we all know that in the end, anytime you take a "shortcut" in life for instant gratification, there is always going to be a high price to pay. You're playing a HUGE game of risk when you're dabbling around in the area of sexuality that will lead to severe sexual brokenness. Not only STDs and unplanned pregnancies, but emotional scars that you will carry for the rest of your life and will require major healing down the road.

Even though the topic of "junk" for today says "premarital sex," I want to be clear in addressing the things listed in the opening paragraph. Pornography, erotica novels (which we discussed more in depth in Day 2), oral sex, homosexuality/bisexuality, and all the way to sexual intercourse are all in the same category of pre-marital sex. We somehow think we have the right to redefine God's gift of sex and put certain actions in subcategories, but the bottom line is that it is all the same. It robs us of the purity of our heart, mind, and body that God desires for us to have and reserve as a gift to share COMPLETELY and SOLELY with our spouse someday!

We've got to quit believing the lie from the enemy that we're missing out if we don't surrender to the temptations around us and that it's okay to give in because that's just the culture we live in today. It's a lie from the ultimate liar himself, and it's time we step up and begin to possess some self-control in the area of sexuality.

God is not saying "No, No, No" when it comes to sex for you...He's just saying "Not yet!"

DIY:

Re-Think (Journal & Pray):

+ Ask God to help you be strong when it comes to sexual temptations and pressures. Use this time to confess to the Lord any sexual sins that you may have in your life.
+ Allow some time for the Holy Spirit to minister to your heart and begin the healing process of restoring self-control in your life in the area of sexual temptation.
+ Take some time to pray and reflect on any current relationships that may need to end because you have the inability to abstain from sexual temptations.
+ Guidelines are huge in order to reach today's goal of repossessing self-control! CLEAR boundaries needs to be set in order to prevent further heartbreak in the area of purity.

Re-Visit the Word:

+ Proverbs 5:20-23
+ Song of Songs 2:7

Re-Claim:

In small group or with your accountability partner, discuss the following: What do you believe the Bible teaches about sex? What are the areas where you need help in staying sexually pure? How do you think God feels about your sexual choices? What aspects of your sexual life do you see as being unhealthy? What behaviors have you changed in order to prevent committing the same mistakes again? Have you experienced guilt from mistakes related to your sexual choices?

Day Five

JUNK: DESTRUCTIVE WORDS

> Do not let any unwholesome talk come out of your mouths, but only what is helpful for building others up according to their needs, that it may benefit those who listen. **Ephesians 4:29** (NIV)

> For out of the overflow of the heart the mouth speaks. **Matthew 12:34b** (HCSB)

When was the last time you were tempted to walk out of a movie or change a song because of the bad language you were listening to? The level of your sensitivity to destructive words and trashy talking has most likely dropped dramatically in the last few years. Although there are many contributing factors to this, one you have the most control over is your exposure and reaction to it. There is an old saying that goes like this: "garbage in-garbage out." It has been proven true time and time again, especially in the arena of our thoughts and words. Think about it.

When you allow and even pay good money to surround yourself with negative, trashy, destructive talking you are taking garbage in, and guess what that means? Matthew 12:34b says, "For out of the overflow of the heart the mouth speaks." Garbage will be what comes out of your mouth when it is what you continually take in. You're probably wondering or thinking, "Why does it even matter? If everyone else talks like that then why shouldn't I?" Good question.

After all we live in this world and have to relate to it all the time, so why then should we worry about sounding different than everyone else? We are supposed to be holy because God is holy. I love what Peter says: "As obedient children, do not be conformed to the desires of your former ignorance. But as the One who called you is holy, you also are to be holy in all your conduct; for it is written, Be holy, because I am holy" (1 Pet. 1:14-16, HCSB).

That cuts to the heart of the matter pretty well. Are you willing to continue living in ignorance or do you want to grow up and be more effective for the Kingdom? If you do then it will affect every area of your life including your speech. Girls—it's time to grow up and learn to stand for TRUTH, and that means refusing to allow trash-talking into your life or out of your mouth—whether that is cursing, negative talk, or calling your good friend trashy names in "fun." If it isn't uplifting or encouraging you don't need to say it. Period.

Ephesians 4:29 says to let NO unwholesome word come out of your mouth. It is displeasing to God and not a good witness. This kind of junk may be the hardest to remove because it is so prevalent, but as you pray about it and choose to be intentional with what you allow into your mind and out of your mouth, you will see a huge difference...best of all you will be a better witness for Him.

DIY:

Re-Think (Journal & Pray):

+ Honestly evaluate your speech. Do you sound more like the world or a Christ-follower?
+ How well do you live up to the Ephesians 4:29 instruction?
+ Confess the ways you have willingly submitted yourself and invited trash-talking into your mind.
+ Ask the Lord to convict you and strengthen you to stand against the current culture and refuse to surround yourself with negative, trashy talking.

Re-Visit the Word:

+ Psalm 19:12-14
+ Memorize: Psalm 19:14

Re-Claim:

In small group or with your accountability partner, discuss the following: Why do we so easily allow ourselves to talk in ways that aren't pleasing to God? How does the way you talk affect your witness negatively or positively? What will you do to change the garbage you are allowing into your life?

5

PROJECT:

Regain Strength

Be strong and very courageous. Be careful to
obey all the law my servant Moses gave you;
do not turn from it to the right or to the left,
that you may be successful wherever you go.
Joshua 1:7 (NIV)

Who is the bravest person you know? Some of the ones that come to my mind are people who are facing very tough life challenges, either physically or emotionally, and still stand firm in their faith. I remember one of the first terrible school shootings in this country—at Columbine High School in Colorado in 1999. Rachel Scott was one of the students who was killed. Here is a quote from her brother, who was also at the school that day. Scott says that his sister was mocked for her faith and then shot. "The last moment of her life was, Eric picked her up by her hair and said, 'You still believe in God?' And she said, 'You know I do.' And he said, 'Well, go be with Him," then she was shot and killed."[7]

Wow. Do you ever wonder if you would have the courage to speak up for God if you knew it would cost your life? Most of the time the persecution we face in this country is not that extreme, but we do have to deal with plenty of circumstances and situations that can create fear in us. Think about what scares you. How do you handle fear? Do you run from it or hit it head on? Do you dread those things that might scare you so much that you miss out on opportunities? Fear is a normal part of life and something that we all must deal with. The key is for us to move forward in this project and scrape away some junk that weighs us down and wraps us up in fear.

Most things written for girls don't talk much about courage and strength. Those topics have typically been reserved for the guys. But let's be honest—this is a tough world and it can be scary to be a girl these days. That is not an excuse for us to hide out from the world in fear though! We need to learn to be girls and women who stand for God, firm in our faith, no matter what comes against us.

In Joshua 1:7, God instructs Joshua, who was the leader of the Israelites as they were finally ready to take the Promised Land, to "be strong and courageous." You may think, "Well that's easy for them to do. They are in the Bible and part of God's big story." Here's the deal though—there was plenty to strike fear in Joshua and the people he was leading, just as there is plenty in your life that might do the same. Before you write off this lesson as not applying to you, understand that YOU are part of God's story. That means that every bit of this challenge and encouragement is for YOU too!

So, what is the secret of how you can be strong and courageous like Joshua was? Keep reading in verse 7 and you'll see: "Be careful to obey all the law" and "do not turn from it to the right or to the left." The law is the Word of God and He is stressing the importance of knowing the Bible and doing what it says. Too many of us are familiar with the Bible but aren't really living with it as part of our daily lives. If you want to live in victory over the junk of fear, rejection, worry, and other things that weigh you down, then you have to be intentional about knowing AND doing what Scripture says. Then you will be "successful" in everything you do just like Joshua.

Day One

JUNK: FEAR AND ANXIETY

> For God has not given us a spirit of fearfulness, but one of power, love, and sound judgment. **2 Timothy 1:7** (HCSB)

> Do not fear, for I have redeemed you; I have called you by your name; you are Mine. **Isaiah 43:1b** (HCSB)

We have a make-believe world swirling around in our minds daily as girls, the world of the "what-ifs." Fear can be paralyzing. Today we're not talking about scary things that you were frightened of as a child such as strange noises at nighttime, monsters under the bed, or shadows on the wall. We're talking about the kind of fear that can leave us numb when we allow our thoughts to take the reigns and run away from us. If not dealt with, and addressed with the Lord, this issue of fear and anxiety can become so controlling that it takes over and can change our quality of life!

We live in a society full of anti-anxiety medications to help people cope with paralyzing and life-altering fear and anxiety. I'm not saying medications are a bad thing because I definitely think those are necessary for some people, but I do think we've allowed this issue of fear to rule us. Maybe we fear if we are going to make it and succeed in this life. Some of you may fear death or fear something happening to you or your family. Maybe it's a fear of a certain medical diagnosis for you or someone you love. You may fear you'll never find love and that you'll be single the rest of your life. And if we are honest, we would admit that especially as girls, we fear the unknown. We fear it because we can't control it. We have this crazy inner desire to be control freaks. And at the end of the day our desire to want to control things that are out of our control will drive us crazy!

I love the truth from God's Word in today's verse, 2 Timothy 1:7—the reminder that God hasn't given us a spirit of fear! The Greek word translated here for "fearfulness" is a strong term for cowardice, or someone who fled from battle. We all know that God doesn't desire for us to live a cowardly life, so what is the opposite of being cowardice? Boldness. This is a characteristic that is made possible in our lives due to the Holy Spirit in us. When our natural tendency in our flesh is to be cowardice and fearful, God has given us the Spirit to help us achieve boldness and power to face this life, whatever may be just around the corner. God cares so much about us as His children. He alone is sovereign and in control of every situation, and all that He wants is for us to acknowledge Him as such and live in a way where we TRUST Him with our lives. He tells us in Isaiah 43:1b, "Do not fear, for I have redeemed you; I have called you by your name; you are Mine."

When we're fearful or feel those anxious thoughts rising up choking us from within, we are to pray! Communicate to the Lord your fears, what you're struggling through. He has no problem controlling the chaos of our lives. So, if we will simply stop in the moment and acknowledge Him as being God when our moment of fear or anxiety is creeping in, the load will all of a sudden seem a little bit lighter.

When you trust Him...REALLY trust Him...you will see how good He is. He holds the world in His hands; I think He can handle us in our fragile and fearful state.

DIY:

Re-Think (Journal & Pray):

+ Read Isaiah 45:5-7. Take a moment and consider just how huge your God is! Rest in His hands and lay your anxious heart before the Lord!

- Take some time to pray and confess any areas of fear and anxiety that you carry. Release the desire for control in these areas and allow the Lord to lift this weight and help you be freed up from the bondage of fear.
- Journal about the areas of your life that leave you feeling weighed down, that you're fearful of. Write out any thoughts you have about the Lord after reading Isaiah 45:5-7.

Re-Visit the Word:

- 1 John 4:18
- Luke 12:22-36
- Memorize: Isaiah 43:1b

Re-Claim:

In small group or with your accountability partner, discuss areas of your life where you struggle with fear. Where do you think these fears come from? Do you really trust that God is who He says He is? That He is good and sovereign?

Take some time to pray together that God will help you break the bondage of fear and anxiety in your life.

HEALING BROKENNESS:

Although anxiety and fear can seem very irrational to those who are not the ones experiencing it, if you are someone who battles with either of these things, the emotions are very real to you. Our bodies have what is called the "fight or flight" response, which gets engaged when we experience real fear or "perceived fear," and this enables us to fight when we need to fight for our lives or flee if the situation is dangerous. The problem is that we experience the same effects on our body whether or not there is a real need to respond that way or not. Over a period of time when someone's adrenals have to continue to produce adrenaline to give the body the fight or flight response, they eventually grow tired of fighting and people experience a multitude of symptoms. This can cause difficultly with concentrating, sleep, focus, rest, and simply emotional balance.

As a teen, there are many things in life that can be stressful and it is so important to learn how to cope with stress now because the long-term effects can really take their toll! They can even manifest into a more serious diagnosis like anxiety, depression, panic attacks, or even post traumatic stress disorder!

God is the ultimate healer and has the ability to heal anything immediately. But sometimes healing is a process that requires your participation.

Practical Steps Towards Coping with Fear and Anxiety:

+ Recognize it for what it is...awareness is the first step towards change!
+ Remember your body can only physiologically handle so much stress, and you are in charge of reducing that stress!
+ Insert positive coping strategies into your life; i.e.: journaling, reading, running, talking with a friend, deep breathing, prayer, etc.
+ Consider talking with a professional Christian Counselor who can work with you to address possible deeper issues causing you to feel paralyzing stress and anxiety (trauma, abuse, neglect, volatile environments, abandonment, etc.)
+ Remember that diet and exercise play a huge role in our bodies ability to regulate itself. What we eat and how active we are affects our hormone levels, endorphins, and ability to manage stress!
+ Know that you are not alone, and if your body is showing symptoms, it is an outward way of letting you know something inward needs to be dealt with!

Day Two

JUNK: REJECTION

> The LORD your God is with you, he is mighty to save. He will take great delight in you, he will quiet you with his love, he will rejoice over you with singing.
> **Zephaniah 3:17** (NIV)

Remember in elementary school recess when it was time to play kickball or something like that and captains were named to choose teams? There have been movies made about that moment of standing there hoping to be picked and not wanting to be last. When you see people lined up waiting to be chosen it usually causes a clench in your gut because you can empathize with them. No one likes rejection. Everyone wants to be chosen to be on the team, to be asked to the prom, to be invited to the party, to be picked in the group, to be accepted.

But I bet you, along with everyone else reading this, can think of a time when you didn't get picked. When you were the one left out. When you felt the sting of rejection. It stinks, but it is part of life. No one can escape the feeling that goes with being left out for whatever reason. You probably have even thought that when you get older it won't be an issue anymore, but that's not the case. (Sorry!) No matter what age you are, the fear of rejection never goes away for good. That makes it even more important that we learn how to deal with it so that we don't get a lot of build up that will tarnish our identity and affect the way we see ourselves.

Who makes you feel good about yourself because of the way they accept and love you no matter what? Those are the people we love to be with—unfortunately they are not always around. When you struggle with feeling rejected and alone, you will be tempted to believe the lies the world says about you. It is these times that you need to remember and focus on the words of Zephaniah 3:17: "The LORD your God is with you, he is mighty to save. He will take great delight in you, he will quiet you with his love, he will rejoice over you with singing." How COOL is that?

The Lord, the King of Kings, Jehovah the Mighty God takes great delight in you—you are His FIRST pick, and He rejoices over you with singing. Let that sink in...

DIY:

Re-Think (Journal & Pray):

+ What area in your life do you fear rejection most often?
+ List the lies you have believed about your identity because of rejection you have faced.
+ Now write out Zephaniah 3:17 and underline all the things that God says and feels about you. Then draw a line through the lies you wrote earlier.
+ Write out a prayer expressing your thanksgiving at being loved and accepted so fully and completely.

Re-Visit the Word:

+ Memorize: Zephaniah 3:17

Re-Claim:

In small group or with your accountability partner, discuss the following: How have you been involved in rejecting others? What do you need to do differently in light of this lesson? What have you missed out on because you feared rejection? How do you feel when you realize the truth of Zephaniah 3:17? Why is it so important to know that you are unconditionally loved, accepted, and chosen by God? Who else do you know who needs to hear this Truth? Tell them this week about how God loves and accepts them.

Day Three

JUNK: GRUDGES

Hatred stirs up conflict, but love covers over all offenses. **Proverbs 10:12** (HCSB)

We've all experienced some kind of hurt in our lives that feels like we're living a scene straight out of the movie *Mean Girls*. Something was done to us or said about us that stirred up drama and conflict, all as a means for someone else to feel better about herself. You see it played out daily on your school campus, in your group of peers, and even more so on television shows that you watch. It's modeled before us on nearly every show on TV these days, whether it's a reality show, a movie, or a hit show targeted to teen girls.

These girls (and women) have believed the lie that they'll feel better about themselves by putting someone else down or making them feel inferior. However, this mentality always backfires resulting in lots of wounded and hurting people on both sides. We live in a society where we're told that it's "all about me." This "Me-ism"—that says it's all about me, my feelings, and my happiness—is crippling to us as girls. This selfish mentality especially rears its ugly head when we've been wounded by someone, whether a friend or maybe even a family member. Girls who have been hurt begin to harbor hatred towards someone in their heart that, when it's not dealt with, grows into a grudge, and grudges are so unhealthy. Let's talk about the definition of a grudge. A grudge is a lingering feeling of resentment toward someone who caused you insult or injury.

Grudges usually cause a girl to act out and take out their hurt on someone else...thus the saying "hurting people hurt people." Putting others down as a means to make you feel better will never work. Even if you're the one who has been the victim, letting grudges grow and develop in your heart towards someone else will only rub salt into an already open wound of hurt. Holding a grudge never actually deals with the original problem.

Cat-fights, jealousy, back-stabbing, gossip, and drama that all girls experience at one point or another are simply a result of a human heart seeking validation, acceptance, love, and identity in someone or something apart from God. We were created to bring glory to God, but if we're so busy with the drama caused by the grudges we carry, we're not doing a very good job of bringing Him glory!

In order to be freed up from the junk of grudges in your life you have to strip away the hatred that you may have allowed to build up in your heart. Proverbs 10:12 says, "Hatred stirs up conflict, but love covers over all offenses." When you're freed up from the hurt that's been done to you, you're then free to love and focus on the things that are most important in this life. When we don't buy into the lie from the enemy of allowing hatred to stir up conflict but instead choose to love and forgive, it becomes possible to love the unlovable and walk away not being another victim of bullying.

DIY:

Re-Think (Journal & Pray):

+ What grudge have you been holding on to? Have you been guilty of carrying a grudge against someone else because of hurt that was done to you? Have you caused hurt to someone else because of your "Me-ism" in putting someone else down in order to make yourself feel more important?
+ Are there people in your life that need forgiveness?
+ Confess any behaviors, thoughts, or actions to the Lord that have resulted in a grudge and taken away from you bringing glory to Him through your life.

Re-Visit the Word:

+ Proverbs 10:12
+ Luke 6:28

Re-Claim:

In small group or with your accountability partner, discuss the following: What are some action steps that you can take when it comes to mean-girl activity that you encounter at school, on your sports team, or even in your student ministry? Are there other areas where grudges can form in your lives other than in friendships?

Discuss effects of grudges even in family dynamics. There might be issues of deep wounds and hurt caused from unspeakable abuse by a family member or friend that are more than just this "mean girl" mentality that may arise as a result of this chapter. If so, please consult a pastor or even professional help from a Christian Counselor to begin a road to healing—there is nothing wrong with getting the help that we need!

JUNK: WORRY

> Do not be anxious about anything, but in everything, by prayer and petition, with thanksgiving, present your requests to God. And the peace of God, which transcends all understanding, will guard your hearts and your minds in Christ Jesus. **Philippians 4:6-7** (NIV)

What if I flunk that test? What if I don't get a date? What if I gain weight? What if they don't let me in the group? What if people make fun of me? What if the economy gets worse? What if I don't get accepted to that school? What if my parents get a divorce? What if the world ends? Whew! Do any of those thoughts sound familiar?

There's a lot to worry about in this crazy, mixed up, mean old world...except that the Bible is pretty clear about what we are supposed to worry about. NOTHING! Read it for yourself in Philippians 4:6-7: "Don't be anxious about anything." Sounds simple enough, but how many of us really live that way? Probably not too many. Our society is set up to cause worry. Think about it. Technology is one of the big contributing factors in worry. Did I delete that last conversation on my phone? Did my mom see what my boyfriend just texted me? Will my friend post that picture of us even though I told her not to? And that's just about things that you shouldn't be doing anyway. One of the best ways to reduce worry is to live the way that God calls you to in His Word. If you are living under the control of the Holy Spirit and following God's plan for your life then your worries will be significantly fewer. People who don't tell lies, sneak around, disobey their parents, and try to be something they aren't just have less to worry about.

So that's one easy way to lessen worry, but what about the worry that isn't caused by your own actions and choices? Worry about the future, relationships, finances, education, and other people's actions toward you are things that you have little to no control over. The Bible is clear about these things also. Don't worry about ANYTHING, and that really does mean anything. This concept falls into the "easier said than done" category so what we need is some good advice on how to make "no worry" a real part of your life. It's not quite as simple as the favorite scene from *Lion King* where Timon and Pumba encourage a worried, shamed Simba to adopt their "No worries for the rest of your days" philosophy. I wish it were as simple as singing "Hakuna Matata," and although that might help a bit, what will be even better is to learn from the Lord what He says to do instead of worry.

Check out what Philippians says just after we are told not to worry about anything, "but in everything, by prayer and petition, with thanksgiving, present your requests to God." Did you catch that? God tells us not to worry BUT to pray and ask God for help while we thank Him in the process. Wow that really isn't too complicated, and here's the even better part: God always keeps His promises, and the rest of those verses tell you what will happen if you choose not to worry but to pray and ask God—"the peace of God, which transcends all understanding, will guard your hearts and your minds in Christ Jesus." Peace. It's the opposite of worry, and it's what we all need a little more of. Peace. It's a game changer, and all you have to do is TRUST Him for it.

DIY:

Re-Think (Journal & Pray):

+ List the things you are worried about right now.
+ Why do you think worry is an easier response than trusting God and going to Him first?

- Recognize worry for what it is. Confess your sin of worry. Ask the Lord to give you peace instead of anxiety as you trust in Him.
- When Christians choose ungodly behaviors, it causes worry. If you're involved in things you shouldn't be then confess and repent of those right now. Ask God for strength to refuse to do them any longer and for conviction when you do.

Re-Visit the Word:

- Proverbs 12:25
- Matthew 6:25-34

Re-Claim:

In small group or with your accountability partner, discuss the following: If you pray about something before you freak out and stress out over it, how does that change your reaction? Why is worry a sin? What can you do to help each other avoid sinful situations that cause worry and stress? (See Prov. 12:25.)

Pray for each other to have more TRUST and less worry over things that are beyond your control anyway. What is the main message of Matthew 6:25-34, and how does it apply to you today?

JUNK: WORLDLINESS

> Do not love the world or the things that belong to the world. If anyone loves the world, love for the Father is not in him. **1 John 2:15** (HCSB)

As a Christian, we are called to be set apart, to be different than this world. We're living in a day and age where even people within the church, who call themselves Christians, are compromising truth in order to dabble in the pleasures of this world. "Straddling the fence" so to speak, in having one foot towards godliness but one foot still stretching for the world. But girls, we've got to stand strong against the desires of the world.

Our natural bent and tendency in our flesh is to gravitate to the pleasures this world offers because they are alluring, they are appealing...but they are sin. And it's important to recognize sin for what it is, and as a believer it is contrary to how the Lord desires for us to live. When we begin to love the world and the things of this world more than we love and desire godliness, it opens our lives up to compromise. We begin to compromise more areas of our convictions and beliefs as a means to fit in with the world, and we're then compromising the grace that Jesus died to give us.

In 1 John 2:15, John is warning us not to LOVE this world or the things it offers us! We know that we live in a sinful world that is in desperate need of a Savior, but we are not to be OF the world, meaning we're not to partake in the pleasures that this world offers. There is no way to daily be exposed and influenced by a culture far from God and not be affected by it. We are to be set apart!

One New Testament commentary on this passage states that "during this time Christianity was rejected and Christians were persecuted. However, as persecution began to subside, John was warning against the temptation to become relaxed in belief and practice. He was also warning against the lax attitude about sin taught by the false teachers."[8]

This can definitely be used to describe our society today. We're not living in a culture that experiences persecution of believers of Jesus Christ, as in other parts of the world, just yet. But our society is increasingly hostile towards Christian beliefs. You are in a very impressionable and formative stage in your beliefs and if you're not careful you will be influenced by the wrong ideals from this world. Again, it goes back to the truth that there is a real enemy out to steal, kill, and destroy your life and all the good that God intends for you!

It's so easy to go with the flow of our culture and what it dictates as important and relevant all the while leaving the truth of God and His Word in hindsight. Then before you know it you've abandoned your faith all for a lax attitude about sin and relaxed view of your beliefs. And this is a tremendously scary place to be! If you continue on a road seeking the fleeting pleasures of this world, you will find yourself wasting a life that God intended for eternal purposes!

Girls, we are supposed to look different from this world. We are to strive after godliness instead of worldliness, and despite what you've heard, it's a GREAT thing! It's what sets us apart as a daughter of the King, and at the end of the day, it is what will last forever!

DIY:

Re-Think (Journal & Pray):

+ Really take some time to reflect on your life as a believer. Use this time to confess any thoughts or actions where you followed hard after worldliness and compromised your convictions instead of pursuing godliness.
+ Ask yourself these questions: Are you someone who tends to go with the flow and follow the crowd? Or do you stand up holding to your convictions from God's Word? Are you allowing yourself

to be influenced by the culture? In what ways? How are you leveraging your influence for the gospel with those around you?

✦ Take time to journal about some intentional life goals—have a plan of action in place so you won't find yourself "straddling the fence" spiritually.

Re-Visit the Word:

✦ 1 John 2:15-17

Re-Claim:

In small group or with your accountability partner, review some of the "Re-Think" questions listed above and discuss. Is godliness really all that important? Why or why not? What are areas that are compromised by believers in today's society that we need to stand stronger on?

6

PROJECT:

Retrieve Peace

Therefore, as God's chosen people, holy and dearly loved, clothe yourselves
with compassion, kindness, humility, gentleness and patience. Bear with
each other and forgive one another if any of you has a grievance against
someone. Forgive as the Lord forgave you. And over all these virtues put on
love, which binds them all together in perfect unity.
Colossians 3:12-14 (NIV)

I magine that you were just invited to the coolest event. It can be whatever works for you. As you celebrate and squeal with joy, what is the next thought that typically hits you? "WHAT am I going to wear?" This question may be one of the most challenging and frequent ones that we deal with. Sometimes I get so forgetful, or tired of trying to think of what outfits I like in my closet, so I found an app for my phone that stores pics you take of your outfits and reminds you of good choices. I know— extreme—but anything to save myself some time and frustration, right?

Whether you are as bad as me or not, every one of us deals with the issue of "what to wear." It's also wise to consider the flip side of the question. You've probably seen the popular show based on this concept called "What Not to Wear." On that show the fashion experts secretly film an unsuspecting person to see what kind of style she has. Then they surprise her with an offer of a whole new wardrobe if she will learn from their style expertise and change her pathetic or inappropriate ways. It's always interesting to watch someone struggle with being willing to break her bad clothing habits in order to get the new clothes.

I bet you are seeing the spiritual parallel at this point. Colossians 3:12-14 gives a clear picture of what you should be wearing every day. Look at what is listed: "clothe yourselves with compassion, kindness, humility, gentleness and patience." Wow, good list. I wonder how many of us are intentionally putting those characteristics on each day? Not too many, or the number of gals who can honestly say that they are at peace would be much higher. This week we want to talk about some of the "junk" that is hindering you from retrieving peace and living in it daily.

The world is affecting your wardrobe, not just physically but spiritually and emotionally too. Instead of living with compassion, gentleness, and patience, most of us are frustrated, impatient, and irritated. What we need to do is follow the very WISE instruction from the Word of God that includes bearing with each other, forgiving, and choosing love as our overarching motto. You may have noticed that the specific characteristic mentioned are also found in Scriptures that list the fruit of the Spirit (Gal. 5:22-23). That's one of the coolest things about the Word of God; it backs itself up and reminds you of things God already told you somewhere else.

So think about this: as you choose your outfit each day, why not put on the fruit of the Spirit? That way you can be clothed beautifully INSIDE and out. Now read John 16:33 to see what will happen when you choose to clothe yourself spiritually: "I have said these things to you, that in me you may have peace. In the world you will have tribulation. But take heart; I have overcome the world" (ESV).

PEACE. That's what can be yours...

Day One

JUNK: ANGER

> Understand this, my dear brothers and sisters: You must all be quick to listen, slow to speak, and slow to get angry. Human anger does not produce the righteousness God desires. **James 1:19-20** (NLT)

I don't know if you've noticed it or not, but girls are rather emotional creatures. We're especially emotional when we've been hurt or feel that someone has wronged us, and we respond or "lash out" in anger.

Anger, although it is a common emotion in girls, can also be very dangerous and toxic for our souls. God knows that we will have times when we get angry, but it's what results from our anger that becomes sin. Ephesians 4:31 and Colossians 3:8 describe anger when it turns to fits of rage, bitterness, brawling, slander, malice, and filthy language. It's what we do with our anger that will either make or break us. James challenges us in James 1:19 as his sisters to understand this: "You must be quick to listen, slow to speak, and slow to get angry."

Quick to listen: How many times do we react to a person or situation without fully listening or hearing that person out? As girls, we tend to be reactors and jump to attack at the smallest threat. I also can't help but wonder if we'd truly be quick to listen, how much time and heartache it would save us and keep us from losing our cool.

Slow to speak: Oh my word, girls...we could camp out here all day! To be a girl who has the self-control to be slow to speak. Now, that would be a modern-day miracle. In order to retrieve and take back peace in our lives, we must learn to control these mouths of ours. So, next time before you react and spout off with a verbal reaction, take a minute, stop, and think through what your response SHOULD be, not what you WANT to say.

Slow to get angry: Now girls, this is where things get really tricky and can truly only be the Holy Spirit at work in us. Peace is only found through the Holy Spirit in our lives, so without Him, being slow to anger is impossible. But for a girl who has the Holy Spirit living in her, this is definitely a possibility. When you open your heart for the Holy Spirit to take the reins of each day of your life and even recognize when you need to hand control back over throughout the day, you can begin to abide in the peace He desires for your life.

There were times during Jesus' earthly ministry when the religious leaders of His day tried to provoke Him. In most circumstances, He responded with a gentle answer and used a "turn the other cheek" approach. There was an instance, however, when Jesus did display a righteous anger in the temple court. John 2:13-17 tells us that Jesus drove out the impurity from His Father's house when He saw the market that had been created to make a profit off those coming to worship. Even today, there are times when Christians need to display a righteous anger in response to the injustice around us. When we see something being done that breaks the heart of God it should stir something within us. That's the Spirit of God moving us to action. Just remember, this is the only type of anger that honors God.

In every circumstance, think about the consequences of your actions before you respond. Challenge yourself to listen, be slow to speak, and in turn be slow to anger...for "human anger does not produce the righteousness God desires."

DIY:

Re-Think (Journal & Pray):

+ What area from James 1:19 do you need to work on the most in order to have a more "peaceful" spirit? Ask the Holy Spirit to help strengthen you in these areas.
+ When was the last time you were angry? What caused it?

+ Journal about any anger that you are currently harboring in your heart that is unhealthy and can result in bitterness, rage, jealousy, or envy.
+ Are you harboring anger against anyone who has hurt you?

Re-Visit the Word:

+ Galatians 5:19-26
+ Ephesians 4:26 and 31
+ Colossians 3:8
+ Proverbs 14:29
+ Ecclesiastes 7:9
+ Memorize: James 1:19-20

Re-Claim:

In small group or with your accountability partner, discuss the following: Are there areas of your life where you struggle with anger? Are there instances where you should have *righteous* anger against injustice in our world and be moved to take action? How can you apply today's truths in your life?

If anger is an issue for you, ask for some accountability and memorize some of the Scriptures above. These verses will help you when you struggle with your temper.

Day Two

JUNK: FRUSTRATION WITH RELATIONSHIPS

> Be in agreement with one another. Do not be proud; instead, associate with the humble. Do not be wise in your own estimation. Do not repay anyone evil for evil. Try to do what is honorable in everyone's eyes. If possible, on your part, live at peace with everyone. **Romans 12:16-18** (NIV)

Who really gets on your nerves? Don't say any names out loud, but truthfully, we all have people who are…ummm...challenging for us to enjoy. Even the best of relationships can cause irritation or frustration at times. Here's another question for you to consider: When you are frustrated with a certain person or relationship, how do you handle it? Do you avoid, ignore, or take your frustration out on that person? Have you ever tried to get to the root of the issue between the two of you and work it out?

Let's consider how God would have us handle hard relationships. Passages like Romans 12:16-18 give us truth that is easier said than done. In fact, the only way we can handle relationships with grace is by the power of the Holy Spirit working in and through us. You see, that flesh nature of ours tends to react to frustration with more, shall we say, ungodly characteristics, unless we are intentional about choosing the right response. And we see from this passage that the right response is to humble ourselves, focus on things we can agree on, extend mercy, do what is honorable, and look for ways to live at peace with everyone we know.

Think about this. If you give in to the temptation to be frustrated, what is the most likely outcome? Well, any number of sins can result. Talking bad about that person behind her back, talking bad about that person to her face, using social media to express your anger, giving mean and nasty looks—you get the picture. It isn't pretty!

Hebrews 12:14 tells us to "Make every effort to live in peace with all men and to be holy; without holiness no one will see the Lord" (NIV). Don't miss that last part. When you give in to the flesh, you miss the opportunity to display the beauty of holiness. God gave us relationships as a gift, not a source of frustration. And when we look to Him, He will give us the grace to love others well...even those who are harder for us to get along with!

DIY:

Re-Think (Journal & Pray):

+ List some things that are causing frustration in your relationships.
+ How do you usually react to relational struggles?
+ Confess any evil thoughts, words, or actions you have expressed toward others that were not honoring to God.
+ Ask God to help you resist the temptation to give in to sin in those difficult relationships.

Re-Visit the Word:

+ Romans 12:16-18

Re-Claim:

In small group or with your accountability partner, discuss the following: What are some things you have learned as a result of difficult relationships? How has God shaped your character through those experiences? How often do you pray for the people you have trouble getting along with?

Romans 12:16-18 gives us several challenges in how we are to handle relationships. Which of these godly responses is the most difficult for you in your current relationships?

HEALING BROKENNESS:

Sometimes I think if people lived on islands by themselves, then there would never be any issues! The problem is we do not live on islands, we live in community, we work with people, we go to school with people, we have to do projects with people, and most of all we are in relationship with people. I love the Scripture that says, "As iron sharpens iron, so one person sharpens another" (Prov. 27:17, NIV).

This Scripture is often used in counseling married couples because they tend to forget that God brings people together for an eternal purpose. His desire in all relationships (marriages and friendships) is that we would bring out the best in one another and challenge each other to become all He created us to be. When we forget that God can use relationships to sharpen us, we tend to become dull and end up provoking one another.

Ask yourself the following questions:
+ Is the common denominator of all your relational problems you?
+ Are you quick to walk away from a friendship when its not going how you want it to?
+ Do you display passive aggressive behaviors such as talking behind someone's back rather than confronting them head on?
+ Is it really the people you are frustrated with, or is it something else? Is something deeper going on?

Practical Steps towards Overcoming Frustration in Relationships:
1. Learn the skill of appropriate confrontation: i.e., say to the person, "I like you and think you are great; however, I did not like when you did…" Separate the person from what they did, and understand it is not them you do not like but their behavior.
2. Recognize that God puts people in your life to shape you, sharpen you, and help you become who you are meant to be. Embrace it rather than fight it!
3. Before dealing with a problem, take some time to calm down, pray, and gather your thoughts. Sometimes people are not ready to hear what you have to say, even if it is something in them that needs to change. It is the Holy Spirit who has to reveal to you a good time to confront, and it should be done in love, not in anger.
4. Be quick to forgive, and remember every friendship is an opportunity to honor God!

Day Three

JUNK: FRUSTRATION WITH GOD

Dear brothers and sisters, when troubles come your way, consider it an opportunity for great joy. For you know that when your faith is tested, your endurance has a chance to grow. So let it grow, for when your endurance is fully developed, you will be perfect and complete, needing nothing. **James 1:2-4 (NLT)**

Do you "pout" or get frustrated when things don't seem to go your way? Maybe it's a situation that you thought should have gone a different way, or you lost someone close to you and do not see or understand the "why." As believers, we sometimes tend to shift that frustration from not understanding back at God. We begin to doubt God's goodness and doubt if He really is there and in control. Feeling frustrated with God is a normal emotion as a human being. All throughout Scripture we see real people who have real feelings and take it out with a real God. Just look at the lives of people like Sarah, Job, Jeremiah, King David, Jonah, or even Martha—the list goes on and on.

Let's take a closer look today into the life of Job. No person in all of God's Word had more reason to be frustrated at God than him. Many times in the book of Job, he has a brutally honest, emotional, crying out to God kind of moment. Let's look at one of those moments in Job 30:20-23: "I cry to you, O God, but you don't answer. I stand before you, but you don't even look. You have become cruel toward me. You use your power to persecute me. You throw me into the whirlwind and destroy me in the storm. And I know you are sending me to my death—the destination of all who live" (NLT).

It's okay for us to be honest with the Lord in how we feel and what we're walking through. God can totally handle your questions and frustrations. Job knew that he was experiencing a grueling and frustrating test here on earth. But despite His frustration, he never cursed God and never doubted God's sovereignty.

It's important for us to see that most of the time our frustrations stem from our lack of understanding—not from any lack on God's part. We don't always understand why God does the things that He does, but we have to trust Him. That's what faith is all about. We also need to understand that pain in our lives is not necessarily a bad thing. Many times when we're walking through a difficult season of life and we feel that God is silent or is allowing hard things to happen to us, it's all for our good. It's to mold us, to shape us, to transform us into who He desires for us to be. Pain is a difficult thing, but it is a healthy thing.

James 1:2-4 tells us to consider it a joy when troubles come our way! I don't know about you, but I rarely think of JOY when I'm walking through a difficult time. But keep reading and James tells us that as we endure the hard times it strengthens our faith and produces endurance and spiritual growth in our lives. God sees seasons of hardship as opportunities for us to grow up. When life gets hard or confusing, it's easy to question why God is allowing those things to happen, but it's not always our right to know why, nor do we have any right to question God's sovereignty or His goodness.

You see, God is perfect. Psalm 18:30 states, "God—His way is perfect; the word of the Lord proves true; He is a shield for all those who take refuge in Him" (ESV). If we believe that, then we should trust in His goodness and know that His ways are perfect, His timing is perfect, and His results are perfect. He sees the end result from our pain, so don't reject the seasons of hardship in your life. It's for your good and for His Glory!

DIY:

Re-Think (Journal & Pray):

+ I once heard author Iva May make a statement that I have not forgotten and I want to end today with it: "God is good, His word is true, and you can absolutely trust Him!" What are your thoughts about that statement?

+ Frustration with God is a very personal issue—one that really needs to be dealt with between you and the Lord. Always be careful in talking with others about something that needs to be dealt with one-on-one between you and Him. He already knows it from the very moment and first thought of frustration! Take it to Him.

+ Journal your thoughts on today's "junk." Confess any hard feelings towards the Lord from any hardships you've endured in your life.

+ Take some time to examine your heart. Do you truly believe that God is good, that His word is true, and that you can trust Him? As we allow frustrations with God to reign in our hearts we will never be able to retrieve peace in our lives.

Re-Visit the Word:

+ Memorize: James 1:2-4
+ Psalm 18:30

Re-Claim:

In small group or with your accountability partner, discuss some of the stories from Scripture we mentioned today (Sarah, Job, Jeremiah, King David, Jonah, Martha). As you look at these different accounts, keep in mind that these were real people with real hurts and real frustrations they expressed to God. I challenge you to notice how God's character never changes! What can you learn from these people's lives?

Day Four

JUNK: FEELING MISUNDERSTOOD

> Lord, You have searched me and known me. You know when I sit down and when I stand up; You understand my thoughts from far away. **Psalm 139:1-2** (HCSB)

> Therefore, since we have a great high priest who has passed through the heavens—Jesus the Son of God—let us hold fast to the confession. For we do not have a high priest who is unable to sympathize with our weaknesses, but One who has been tested in every way as we are, yet without sin. **Hebrews 4:14-15** (HCSB)

I was driving down the road the other day and the weirdest things kept happening to me where other cars would pull out in front of me or swerve into my lane without warning. I remember saying to my daughter "Do you think I suddenly have the super power of being invisible?" Although there aren't really any super powers aside from the movies, there are times when you might be able to relate to feeling as if no one is seeing you.

I wonder if you have ever felt invisible or misunderstood to the point that you "might as well be invisible." Even though this is a crowded world we live in, things happen sometimes that cause us to feel as if no one really knows or understands us. Even though it's a common feeling, it can be a lonely and tough time. Check out Psalm 139:1-2. Your God, the King of Kings, knows your EVERY single thought—even the one you just had! That's incredible if you consider the number of thoughts you have in a day and the number of people on the planet. That characteristic of God is called "omniscient" and it means "all knowing." I love that there is nothing that escapes God's attention. He NEVER sleeps on the job and is never too busy for you—EVER.

What does it say to you that God knows your every thought and pays attention even when you feel like no one else does? It should be a reminder to you of how much He LOVES you and how valuable you are to Him. Once again we come to a subject where in reality people will let you down. Even people who honestly love you will sometimes be busy when you are trying to talk to them or reading their texts instead of responding to your conversation. They will even at times not notice your sad face and ask you what went wrong with your day. Remember, they are just humans, and it is part of their nature to not be perfect (it's part of yours too) so cut them some slack and take it to God. He is always there for you and knows your every thought and action.

Now, read Hebrews 4:14-15 and see something else really cool about Jesus. Not only does He know you and care about you, but He can also sympathize with you. In other words—He knows how you feel experientially. He knows what it is like to be let down by close friends (can you say Peter?), and He knows what it's like to be betrayed by those closest to Him (what about Judas?). He also knows what it is like to be punished unfairly—ummm perfect, sinless living for 33 years then has the weight of all the sin of all the world on His shoulders—NOT fair, but necessary for us to be saved. And sometimes there is a bigger plan working out around you in your own suffering. What we have to do is trust that God has a plan and He is working it out.

When you feel invisible, betrayed or like life is unfair—HE sympathizes with you. Take your worries and frustrations to Him and get help from the One who knows.

DIY:

Re-Think (Journal & Pray):

+ When have you felt invisible or misunderstood lately?
+ How did you respond? In anger, pity party, whining, or what?
+ In light of today's Scriptures, what should be your response?

- Have you ever thought about the fact that Jesus knows your every thought? How does that change things for you?
- Are there some of your thoughts that you are embarrassed for God to know? If so—write out a prayer of confession of those thoughts now.
- Ask the Lord to remind you of His omniscience when your thought-life leads you in the wrong direction.

Re-Visit the Word:

- Hebrews 4:14-15

Re-Claim:

In small group or with your accountability partner, discuss the following: Why are your thoughts so hard to control? What can you do to better handle the times you feel misunderstood or invisible? If your thought life is allowed to run wild and lead into a big ole pity party then what might happen next?

All sin starts as a thought. Notice the progression: thoughts lead to words, actions, or behaviors. How can it benefit you to apply 2 Corinthians 10:5 to your thought life?

Day Five

JUNK: INSTANT GRATIFICATION

> Wait patiently for the LORD. Be brave and courageous. Yes, wait patiently for the LORD. **Psalm 27:14** (NLT)

Have you heard the phrase that we live in a "microwave" or a "drive-thru" society? Think about it. We have every option of food available at our disposal to drive through and pick up at a window, all without having to get out of our car. We have smart phones and iPods that function as mini-computers where we can download apps or music at the touch of a button. We have e-readers where we can download a book right to our device without having to go to the local bookstore. It's kind of crazy when you stop and think about it. Take the Internet for example, many of us are not very patient when it comes to getting online. We get so impatient if our Wi-Fi connection takes more than 15 seconds to connect! Let's face it...we want things done our way, when we want it, and we need it right now!

More often than not, this lack of patience and sense of instant gratification is how we relate to the Lord in our relationship with Him. We want things to work out and go according to our plans. Just like when a child throws a temper-tantrum because they know what they want and they're going to let you know about it! We are no different with God. Now given, we may not be laying on the floor in the middle of Target kicking and screaming because we want a new Barbie, but we can act very similarly before the Lord in our spiritual life. Spiritually, we're kicking and screaming and throwing a tantrum before the Lord. Maybe we feel like He's not answering our prayers as quickly as we think it should happen, when in all reality we're just not fond of the idea of waiting for anything...even an answer from the Lord.

Let's take a look at the opposite of instant gratification, which is "deferred or delayed gratification." The definition of deferred gratification is resisting temptation for an immediate reward and waiting for a later reward. If we look into God's Word we find many verses, especially in the book of Psalms, where God challenges us to "Be still and know that I am God" (Ps. 46:10, NIV) or "Wait patiently for the LORD. Be brave and courageous. Yes, wait patiently for the LORD" (Ps. 27:14, NLT).

The bottom line is that peace can come in the waiting. It's in the seasons of testing when we get to know our God better. When we delay the desire for instant gratification, this is when spiritual maturity takes place. You see...God's not in a hurry. He sees the big picture of our lives and we don't. He knows what's best for us because He's had our lives planned since the beginning of time. We just need to rest in the fact that God isn't as concerned with meeting our immediate desires as He is our personal growth as His daughters. We will also discover He's not holding out on us...He wants us to hold out for something better...He wants us to desire His best!

DIY:

Re-Think (Journal & Pray):

+ Do you find that your sense of instant gratification has carried over into the demands you place on the Lord?
+ How do you respond when you don't get your way? Do you ever get impatient waiting on the Lord to come through? Journal your thoughts.
+ Take some time to "Be still and know that He is God" today. In your stillness before Him, He can reveal a whole lot to you about who He is, and in the stillness you just might find an answer to something you've been praying for.

+ If you've been praying for something for a while and feel like He hasn't answered, don't give up and throw in the towel. Keep praying until you know He'll give you a yes or a no. Sometimes we take God's pauses for a no when He's just saying "wait."

Re-Visit the Word:

+ Psalm 5:3
+ Psalm 27:14
+ Psalm 31:24
+ Psalm 33:20
+ Psalm 37:7
+ Psalm 38:15
+ Psalm 46:10
+ Romans 8:25

Re-Claim:

In small group or with your accountability partner, discuss the following: What areas of your life do you find you expect instant gratification? How does this mentality affect your life spiritually? Your prayer life?

Discuss areas where you constantly struggle with instant gratification and entitlement. Maybe you need someone to hold you accountable in this area. If so, ask for a fellow believer to come alongside you and help you overcome this. Do you desire for more of a sense of peace in your life? It might be a good idea for you to decide together to take a day once a week or a few times a month to abstain from something—maybe media, music, television, computer time, or maybe your cell phone (GASP!) for a day in order to eliminate the noise and distractions and be still before the Lord.

Recapture Devotion

Love the Lord your God with all your
heart, with all your soul, with all your
mind, and with all your strength.
Mark 12:30 (HCSB)

What does it mean to be devoted to something or someone? You can be devoted to a relationship, a job, a sport, music, or anything because it is something or someone that you focus on, spend time and money on, and make a priority. For instance, most of you are devoted to your cell phone or technology device that keeps you connected. It's your lifeline so if something happens to it you are ready to do whatever it takes to get it back.

One time I was out of town and my son, who was in high school, had his new iPhone disappear from school. It was crazy and we went to great lengths to find that phone. Because I had the "Find My Phone" app on my phone, they were calling me, and I was giving instructions to track the phone. We finally identified that it was at a house in a neighborhood. So my husband and my son went to try and retrieve the phone, but when they got to the house listed, no one was home. After calling in some other reinforcements for information they left some phone messages then decided to try back later. When they went back it turns out that an older couple lived there who didn't even know what an iPhone was. In the process, we learned that the GPS tracking signal is not pinpoint accurate so they proceeded to look in the woods behind the house. Then it started raining. They had a police friend with them who was helping search and people in other houses were even helping. Whew, that's a lot of work to find one little phone. A big storm came in so they didn't find it that night and had to quit without it. The next day that the man and his son who were helping them look called because it "turned up" in the son's backpack, and they heard the alerts we sent to the phone. He said someone put it there as a joke—we were just glad to get the phone back regardless. It was a huge ordeal and took a lot of effort.

I would say that we highly regarded that phone. We were willing to be inconvenienced and change our schedules to find the phone. My son was motivated because he did NOT want to be without his cell phone and had waited a long time to get an iPhone. My husband was motivated because he knew the value of money and how much it would take to replace that phone. You would probably be the same way because technology is important to us. So whether you have a phone, iPhone, iPad, iPod Touch, or whatever, if it connects you to the world, it is valuable.

I wonder why we aren't as diligent and zealous about our devotion to God? We seem much more dedicated and concerned with our things or our "peeps" than we are about time with our Lord and Savior. Then we're shocked when we aren't living in power and freedom. It's actually very simple; if you want to grow in your relationship with the Lord, you need to be DEVOTED to Him. That means spending time and energy on Him and being focused on things that will enable you to be the girl or woman He has called you to be. We only have a certain amount of time and energy to spend, and you will find that you use it up on what is important to you. This week we will talk about some of the "junk" that steals our devotion away from the Lord and what we can do to get it back on track. Jesus Himself told us the most important thing to do is to "love the Lord your God with ALL your heart, with ALL your soul, with ALL your mind, and with ALL your strength." That is a great description of devotion, and one that we need to strive toward on a daily basis. This is a big week...

JUNK: MISPLACED AFFECTIONS

> Set your minds on what is above, not on what is on the earth.
> **Colossians 3:2** (HCSB)

There are many things in this world that we chase after to fill a void, feel fulfilled, and feel validated. It's so easy in this world, living in our flesh, to run after so many things that in the end leave us empty. But Christ is the one true affection that will last. Christ is the only one who has given His very own life for us! That's some pretty amazing love if you ask me! It's more than just some empty words or empty promises given by some ordinary guy. Boys, friendships, sports, popularity, materialism, money—all bide for our affection in this world. And more often than not, we're so quick to give in to those things and turn our affection away from our Savior. Affection means to have a fond attachment, devotion, or love for someone. So let me ask you today, where have you placed your affections? What are you chasing after other than your Savior?

In Colossians, Paul addressed the issue of misplaced affection because he knew this reality to be true—whatever we set our hearts and minds on is what we will chase after. If we are honest, it's easy to become fascinated with the things of this earth, but it's crucial for us to stop and be reminded that our loving and gracious God is also a jealous God. He commands us to not place anything or anyone else in the place where He alone should sit on the throne of our hearts. In Exodus 20:3-5a God says, "Do not have other gods besides Me. Do not make an idol for yourself, whether in the shape of anything in the heavens above or on the earth below or in the waters under the earth. You must not bow down to them or worship them; for I, the LORD your God, am a jealous God" (HCSB). This means that He is serious that our devotion be given exclusively to Him. You may not think that you're worshiping any "idols" in your life, but an idol is not just some stone-carved or golden image. It's anything that you've placed in your life that means more to you than God—that thing or person that if you lost it, you'd feel as if your life was over. You see girls, we were all created to worship something. And this space that we have in our hearts was created for affection and devotion to be given to the Creator. He should be the only one to reign on the throne of our hearts.

When we misplace this affection designed for Him with other things that this world says is of value, we lose. Look at the wise words from King Solomon, a man who in the world's eyes had everything and lacked nothing. In Ecclesiastes 1:14 he wrote, "I observed everything going on under the sun, and really, it is all meaningless—like chasing the wind" (NLT).

Misplacing our affection for the Lord by placing value on the things of this world is like "chasing the wind." So if you've found yourself caught up in trying to win the approval of people rather than God, God's desire is for you to return wholeheartedly to Him. Our religion and service aren't enough—God's wants all of our hearts and affection for Him and Him alone!

DIY:

Re-Think (Journal & Pray):

+ What are some things that have competed with your affection for the Lord? Take some time to think, pray, and journal through your life. Examine your heart and ask the Lord for forgiveness for worshiping "other gods" in your life.

- What are some of the things that you "worship" in your life? Have you found fulfillment and purpose in those things? Or do you recognize that you have a void in your heart that only Jesus can fill?
- If you feel you're at a place in your relationship with Him that has grown stale or stagnant, come back to Him.

Re-Visit the Word:

- Exodus 20:3-5a
- Deuteronomy 5:8-10
- Memorize: Deuteronomy 6:5

Re-Claim:

In small group or with your accountability partner, discuss the "idols" in your life that you've misplaced your affection on. Why do you think we struggle with "worshiping" things from this world, seeking for those things to fill the void that only God can fill? Have you ever thought about the fact that God is a jealous God? Why does He require our undivided hearts? What are some things that need to change in your life and in your devotion to Him?

JUNK: INSINCERE WORSHIP

> These people honor me with their lips, but their hearts are far from me.
> They worship me in vain; their teachings are but rules taught by men.
> **Matthew 15:8-9 (NIV)**

Have you ever talked to someone and although they said something nice you felt like they didn't mean it? For instance, you know when someone is complimenting you and they aren't being sincere. Maybe they are saying that you look cute and stylish, but their eyes are saying, "Where did she get that and why is she wearing it?" The mouth is saying one thing, but the facial expression, eyes, or body language is saying something entirely different. It makes me feel icky and uncomfortable when I encounter those people because I never know whether I can trust what I hear from them.

Even if someone gets good at controlling their expressions and faking their intentions, insincerity can still shine through and you won't trust them. Christians especially should be sincere and honest people. That doesn't mean that you should go around telling people everything you think about their hair or clothing choices— do all things in love. But you should be sincere and trustworthy. By definition, sincerity means: free from pretense, deceit, or hypocrisy. We have talked about some of those in other days. Today our focus is on what it means to engage in insincere worship, which we need to strip out of our lives.

How is it possible to worship God and not be sincere? One time I was standing and singing along in a worship service. We were lifting up the words "I'm desperate for you" to the Lord and it was like I heard God's voice in my head (He sounded like James Earl Jones), and He said, "Really?!—You're desperate for ME? 'Cause that's not what it looks like from here. From here it looks like you barely have time to fit Me into your busy schedule!" I couldn't sing another word because I was so convicted of the truth—I had gotten very good at going through the motions and doing the right things, but my heart wasn't in it. That, my friends, is insincere worship, and I was guilty of lying to the Lord. When you and I try to worship Him without having our hearts in the right places, we are insincere and full of pretense and deceit. Matthew 15:8-9 says that our lips are saying the right things but our hearts are far from Him. It also says that kind of worship is in vain. It is useless because in essence we are lying to God, and guess what? He KNOWS exactly what we are thinking and feeling and wanting, so when we say or sing "I'm desperate for you," He knows if it's true or not.

The same is true about our prayers. Many of us pray the right things because we have been taught to, but we might not really mean them. If you pray and ask God for help forgiving someone but you don't mean it, He knows—it's powerless prayer. If you bring Him an offering, but you're mad because you could have spent it on yourself, He knows—and it's useless. When these things happen you are just following the rules of men, and your worship is powerless. The key to sincere worship is honesty and truth. You have to start where you ARE. Ask God to help you focus on Him before you get into a worship time. If you're singing and keep getting distracted, stop and pray for focus. If you have a bad attitude about praying for someone or bringing your offering, stop and confess your true feelings to God and then ask Him to change you.

You many think, "I could never tell God what I'm really thinking." I promise—He already KNOWS! He can handle it, and He WANTS you to be honest with Him so that He can unleash His power in your life. Sincere worship is the goal—honestly.

DIY:

Re-Think (Journal & Pray):

+ When have you been guilty of insincere worship lately? Confess those times and ask the Lord to convict you quickly when you start to say one thing even though you mean another, especially in worship.
+ What are some things you know to be true and that you do because you are following the rules of men but your heart isn't really in them? It's time to be honest with the Lord. Confess that you haven't been sincere and ask Him to strengthen your devotion and make your worship pure and sincere in all areas.
+ Some great leaders have said, "It's easier to act your way into a feeling than feel your way into an action." That is also true of us spiritually. The challenge to be sincere in our worship is a reminder that when we continue with the things of God and pray for our hearts to be right then we are on the right track. Pursue sincere worship by continuing to worship and be aware when insincerity creeps in so you can stop it quickly!
+ Write out a prayer of thanksgiving that the Lord loves you enough to want you to be honest with Him and that He gives you complete freedom to tell Him how you really feel with no condemnation—just love.

Re-Visit the Word:

+ Memorize: Psalm 51:10

Re-Claim:

In small group or with your accountability partner, discuss the following: Why do we worship insincerely? When are you most likely to be insincere with the Lord? How can you stop insincerity when it starts happening and focus your worship on something real and honest?

Insincerity is one of the biggest roadblocks to effective prayers (praying is worship). What have you been praying about that you aren't seeing any answers on? Could insincerity be playing a role in how you are approaching God? How can you change your prayer to be more sincere?

Day Three

JUNK: HABITUAL SIN

> So the trouble is not with the law, for it is spiritual and good. The trouble is with me, for I am all too human, a slave to sin. I don't really understand myself, for I want to do what is right, but I don't do it. Instead, I do what I hate.
> **Romans 7:14-15** (NLT)

One of the great struggles for us as believers is that we wrestle with the same sin over and over in our lives. We know what we are supposed to be doing or how we're supposed to respond, but the same issue seems to come up over and over again. For you, it may be the constant struggle with vanity, self-harm, lying, gossiping, a hot temper, sexual activity, or even substance abuse. Whatever it is, if you don't deal with it before the Lord it will steal the abundant life God wants for you. Paul addresses this issue in Romans 7:14-15 where he confirms that the problem is not with the law of the Lord, because it's good and spiritual, the problem is with us! Paul understood the struggle—he wrestled with sin just like we do today, wanting to do what is right but instead doing what he knew was wrong.

You see girls, while we are given a new nature when we enter into a relationship with Christ, our flesh still competes daily with the Spirit inside us. So the question that you must answer is who is going to win this struggle over sin in your life?

There are many believers today who think they can claim Christianity and keep on sinning habitually because "God is gracious, forgiving, and

loving." And that He is! But we're seeing all too often people using this truth as a license to keep on sinning. Those who do this take God's grace and His sacrifice for granted. The authors of *Checkpoints: A Tactical Guide to Manhood* use this analogy: "God's grace doesn't justify your sin any more than wearing your seatbelt justifies you drunk driving."[9] When we talk about "habitual sin," we are talking about the sin you struggle with over and over but justify because of the grace God offers.

Paul asks this question in Romans 6:1-2, "Shall we go on sinning so that grace my increase? By no means! We are those who have died to sin; how can we live in it any longer?" (NIV). His response to the question is a strong NO WAY! We can't go on sinning because if you are a true follower of Jesus Christ, you have died to your flesh and your sinful desires. Let the question that Jesus posed in Luke 6:46 marinate in your heart for a moment, "Why do you call Me 'Lord, Lord,' and don't do the things I say?" (HCSB).

So the question you must ask yourself today if you're struggling with a habitual sin in your life is: Have you truly died to your flesh and the sin that entangles you? You see, there isn't a gray area here. We can't have our cake and eat it too!

DIY:

Re-Think (Journal & Pray):

+ In an attitude of confession, take some time and spend before the Lord. God pours His compassion on us when we are broken over our failures and our sin before Him.
+ Be open to allowing Him freedom to bring healing into your life. Confession of sins is KEY to living a Spirit-filled life. Do you consistently practice confession? If not, begin today.
+ What are some sins that you continue to struggle with that have become "habitual" in your life? Confess the things that the Spirit brings to mind. It may seem small to you but no sin is insignificant in the eyes of our Holy God. Recognizing that we are sinful should lead us to repentance.

+ Another spiritual discipline to begin to put into practice is repentance. Repenting from your sin after confession is making a complete 180-degree turn and walking in the opposite direction!

Re-Visit the Word:

+ Romans 7:14-15
+ Memorize: Luke 6:46

Re-Claim:

In small group or with your accountability partner, ask for accountability as you work to overcome the "habitual sins" in your life. Take a moment and discuss God's grace. Why do you think some believers feel this gives them a license to sin? How can you live differently? Why do we call Him "Lord, Lord" and yet don't do as He says in His Word? Do you think we have a holy fear of our God? Discuss confession and repentance. What do these two spiritual disciplines mean to you?

HEALING BROKENNESS:

In Christian Counseling, we completely rely on the power of God and trust God for healing and breaking patterns; however, a lot of the time, we understand that God asks us to partner with Him to work towards healing and freedom. Habitual sin is a spiritual issue as much as it is an emotional and psychological. The brain carves pathways, and when we do something over and over again, a pathway is created in our brain. So the choice to change that pathway can be very difficult, but definitely possible. Our spiritual journey is constantly one of letting go of the old and embracing the new life in Christ. With the power of the Holy Spirit we are able to break old patterns and adopt new ones that lead us to living a life more holy and pleasing to God.

Romans 12:2 says, "Do not conform to the pattern of this world, but be transformed by the renewing of your mind. Then you will be able to test and approve what God's will is—his good, pleasing and perfect will" (NIV).

Practical Steps:
+ Get in the Word everyday to help renew your mind and line your thoughts with what God has to say.
+ Have people in your life you are close with hold you accountable in the areas that you are weak.
+ Consider talking to a Christian Counselor about possible addictions and destructive thoughts and behaviors, and begin to share what you are struggling with.
+ Keep a thought log so you can begin to be aware of how your thoughts affect your behaviors.
+ Remember that just as easy as your brain carved out negative pathways, it can create new healthy ones! The first few times of making a good choice will seem difficult, but it will get easier with time—and eventually become natural!
+ Reach out to a mentor or leader in your life, and let them know what you are struggling with!

It is not always easy to break negative patterns in your life, but it is definitely possible—and required for the life of a Christian! You can do it, and you will experience so much freedom in Christ when you do!

Day Four

JUNK: INCONSISTENCY

> But thanks be to God! He gives us the victory through our Lord Jesus Christ. Therefore, my dear brothers, stand firm. Let nothing move you. Always give yourselves fully to the work of the Lord, because you know that your labor in the Lord is not in vain. **1 Corinthians 15:57-58** (NIV)

What do you do when something exciting happens? You probably have certain people that you call immediately because, after all, great news is meant to be shared—right? And having someone to squeal and scream about it with you is necessary. That's all good, but think about this: When was the last time you felt excited about spiritual things? Have you ever called a friend to talk about what you learned in the Word or how God spoke to you in your quiet time? Not so much...

For most of us, sometimes it feels like you're taking two steps forward then one step back then three steps to the left and struggling uphill then falling down hill. Let's face it—this journey of being a Christian is NOT boring and it's rarely the same. Just when you get one thing down, something new comes along or you get busy with life and suddenly you find you are struggling with something that never used to be an issue.

If we were all together I would ask you to raise your hand if you ever feel dissatisfied with where you are spiritually. And my hand would be in the air too! Here's the deal, it is difficult to remain consistent in your walk with Christ and that can be frustrating. Now understand when I talk about consistency I don't mean that feeling of being stuck in a rut—that's a lesson for another day. Consistency is about knowing that you are constantly moving forward in your relationship with Jesus. It is all about being dedicated and devoted to Jesus in such a way that you are excited and passionate about Him. Can you imagine having an exciting spiritual life that allows you to live in victory? It's not only desirable—it's possible.

Look at 1 Corinthians 15:57-58 to find some things you can do to become more consistent and start living in victory and power. Where does victory come from? The Lord Jesus Christ. That means that apart from Him you won't be finding it. Keep reading and you'll see some practical advice. Stand firm and let nothing move you. Hmmm...I wonder how many of us are a bit wimpy and easy to sway? Are you that girl who says she is not going to get involved in things that aren't godly and then caves at the first opportunity? Are you the one who acts one way at church and with church friends then totally becomes someone else the minute a cute guy walks in the room? Inconsistencies are going to happen when you aren't prepared to stand firm. I love what Ephesians 6:10-13 says about standing firm. It's all tied to the armor of God and being intentional about putting it on.

Then, as you start standing firm, you've also got the instruction to "give yourself fully to the work of the Lord." This is where many people fall short of experiencing victory in their lives—because they are afraid to dive in whole heartedly to what God wants for them. What if...?

What if you chose to give your all to the Lord today—and tomorrow—and the next day. Imagine what that could be like. How exciting it would be! When you're excited about something, you can't help but share it. And that is exactly what we are called to do.

DIY:

Re-Think (Journal & Pray):

+ What about your spiritual walk is unexciting to you? Why?
+ Make a plan: Don't feel like you have to do the same thing all the time day after day. It is important to have a plan, but you can

mix it up. Try something new for your quiet time. Read through the Bible chronologically, use a different devotional guide, try praying on your knees (literally), journal your prayers. There is no end to what you can do to strengthen your walk with Christ.

Re-Visit the Word:

+ Ephesians 6:13-20
+ Write out the armor of God on a card or your bathroom mirror. Each day this week "pray on" the armor as you are getting ready. Then stand firm.

Re-Claim:

In small group or with your accountability partner, discuss the following: Where do you most struggle with standing firm? How can the armor of God verses help you stand firm? What areas of your walk with Christ are you most inconsistent? What can you do to encourage one another to be consistent in your spiritual walk? Why do you think it matters if you are consistent or not as a Christian? How can keeping your spiritual life consistent and exciting make a difference for Jesus?

Day Five

JUNK: MEDIOCRITY

I have fought the good fight, I have finished the race, and I have remained faithful. And now the prize awaits me—the crown of righteousness, which the Lord, the righteous Judge, will give me on the day of his return. And the prize is not just for me but for all who eagerly look forward to his appearing.
2 Timothy 4:7-8 (NLT)

We expect excellence from ourselves in so many different areas of our lives. Sometimes its even more than just excellence; we put pressure on ourselves for perfection. Our culture paints this picture for us of perfection from magazines, movies, Pinterest, TV commercials, etc.

We obsess over what we think we should look and dress like...how we should do our hair...what fashion is the "in style"...what make-up is the best for our skin tone. But even more than the physical obsession for perfection that we strive to attain, we also pursue excellence in almost every other area of our lives. Maybe in sports, you give 110 percent to be the best on the team. Maybe you strive to find just the right group of friends or the perfect boyfriend. Maybe you pour time and effort in to being at the top of your class. We seek to be the best in all of these areas, but we often keep our spiritual walk and relationship with Jesus on the "back burner." Many Christians settle for a routine of "do's and don'ts" when what we've actually been called to is a more excellent faith.

Our relationship with Jesus Christ for many believers has settled in the dust of mediocrity. We typically don't settle for mediocrity in any other area, but that's what we give the Lord so often. In all reality we should be giving the Lord our VERY best, seeking excellence in our relationship with Him and giving Him our best in this life for His glory and His purpose!

Living a mediocre life is boring, stale, and lifeless. Even the definition of being mediocre is to be inferior in quality or to be plain. Once again, let's look at the life of Paul. In 2 Timothy 4:7-8 Paul is sitting in prison as he writes to Timothy. He gives him some encouragement about how running this "race" of life and giving the Lord 110 percent is totally worth the investment. And just in case you missed it...he's sitting in prison awaiting his SECOND judicial hearing! "I have fought the good fight, I have finished the race, and I have remained faithful. And now the prize awaits me—the crown of righteousness, which the Lord, the righteous Judge, will give me on the day of his return. And the prize is not just for me but for all who eagerly look forward to his appearing."

Sometimes we forget this life is not about us but all about the Lord and His story! We have the privilege and honor as believers in Jesus Christ to be a part of that story. Our spiritual walk should be our first priority. We should give all of the excitement and excellence that our Savior requires of us in EVERY area of our lives, INCLUDING our walk with Him. Girls, it is time that we no longer tolerate being a "mediocre Christian." Our God didn't send His only Son to this earth as a sacrifice to pay the penalty for OUR sin so that you and I can just be ordinary! God doesn't call us to be comfortable, mediocre, ordinary, or boring.

As I'm writing this, I am praying for each of you, that you're heart's desire at the end of all of this is to run hard after Jesus with everything you have. My prayer is that at the end of your life, you can honestly stand before the Lord and say, like Paul, that you have fought the good fight, you finished the race, and you remained faithful!

DIY:

Re-Think (Journal & Pray):

+ Take some time to ask yourself: Have I been living a mediocre life for Jesus? Do I strive for excellence in every other area except my relationship with Him? Confess this to the Lord and ask Him to set your heart so on fire for Him that you can't help but give Him 110 percent!

+ If you've placed other things in your life as more important than your walk with Him, admit it, confess it, and set a plan of action in place to rearrange your priorities. Keep Him first in your life, and I promise you, He will SO honor that choice!

+ Take a moment and really think about what it will be like for you to stand before the Lord some day. What will you tell Him? Will you be able to stand with complete confidence like Paul and say that you have fought...that you finished...and that you remained faithful through it all? If not, what changes need to happen in your heart and in your life so that this will be a reality someday?

Re-Visit the Word:

+ 2 Timothy 3:10-4:8

Re-Claim:

In small group or with your accountability partner, discuss the following: How have you been struggling with the junk of mediocrity? Why do you think Christians settle for being ordinary in their spiritual walk but not in other areas of their lives? What are some changes that need to be implemented in your life to help you move past and strip away this "junk" of mediocrity?

Take some time to pray together for God to do a fresh and mighty change in your heart. Pray the passage out of Jeremiah 20:9 that He would ignite a passion for Him in your life that burns like a fire!

8

PROJECT:

Revive Excitement

They said to each other, "Did not our hearts burn within us while he talked to us on the road, while he opened to us the Scriptures?"
Luke 24:32 (ESV)

What fires you up or really gets you excited? It's not usually too hard to tell when girls are excited about something—as a matter of fact you can typically hear the squealing and screaming from quite a distance. You've probably noticed that females are more emotional creatures (duh), and therefore, we tend to let people know when we are fired up...as long as it is something socially acceptable, that is. What about when it's spiritual?

How would you rate your level of excitement when it comes to your spiritual life? Can you say that your heart is burning within you like we read in Luke 24:32? Honestly, this world can be hard for us to deal with and still keep our passion for God fresh and real. Think about it. Have you ever felt stuck in a rut in your spiritual walk? Most of us have at some time. The good news is that there are things we can learn to deal with so that they won't suck the life out of our passion for God. The "junk" we will talk about this week are all common issues or attitudes that can be like pouring water on a fire. Many times in Scripture you can see the comparison between passion and fire.

There's nothing quite like sitting around a fire, looking into the flames, telling stories, and making s'mores. But there's more to it than that. There is a lot that can be learned from the illustration of fire to help us maintain our passion. Check out what the priests were told in Leviticus 6:12-13, "The fire on the altar is to be kept burning; it must not go out. Every morning the priest will burn wood on the fire. He is to arrange the burnt offering on the fire and burn the fat portions from the fellowship offerings on it. Fire must be kept burning on the altar continually; it must not go out"

(HCSB). Okay. Did you catch that? If you want to keep the fire burning then you have to put wood on it DAILY. Good idea. If you want to keep your fire for God burning brightly then you have to keep adding fuel to it on a daily basis. That's what you've been doing with this book, so stay with it and keep going.

Another lesson about fires that you can apply to your spiritual walk is to notice what happens when one piece of wood is off to the side by itself. The fire on that wood dies out pretty quickly. That illustrates our need to be CONNECTED with other believers. In order to stay burning as brightly as we can we need to be with other Christians. So be committed to your small group, your youth group, your student worship service, and your church.

One last thing about fire before you get into the "junk" of this week. When it's dark outside, what happens to fire? It seems even brighter. A small candle flame can make a huge difference in a dark room, and a campfire can light up the darkest of nights. The world we live in is dark and getting darker so when we as believers are on fire for God, we make a difference that cannot be denied. Keep the fire burning...it's exciting and someone will see and be drawn to it.

Day One

JUNK: APATHY

> But I have this against you: You have abandoned the love you had at first. Remember then how far you have fallen; repent, and do the works you did at first. **Revelation 2:4-5** (HCSB)

Think back to the day when you first surrendered your heart and life to Jesus. Remember the excitement, hope, and peace that was present within your soul. That moment left you feeling excited and empowered, wanting to go and tell everyone you knew about the change He had made in your life. And maybe, once upon a time, that excitement was so apparent to those you encountered. But then over time as the busyness of life, school, schedules, friends, and extra-curricular activities crept in, the excitement began to fade a little bit. Then as you dealt with more issues of peer pressure and the desire to want to be accepted, life pulled you further away until apathy set in and crushed the excitement of the gospel that was once so apparent in your life.

One of the biggest hurdles for this project to revive excitement in our lives, spiritually speaking, is apathy. Apathy means a lack of interest, enthusiasm, or concern. This "junk" is becoming more and more prevalent in the church today. And it's a major issue that we desperately need to strip out of our lives. Spiritually speaking, apathy can be summed up by the lack of interest, enthusiasm, or concern for the things of God. I don't know about you, but that sounds like so many people who claim to be a "Christian" in America today. We all probably know someone who has become disinterested in the things of God, and maybe that someone is you.

When we neglect the simple spiritual disciplines of prayer, reading the Word, being involved in a small group, and worshiping with a local body of believers, why would we expect anything else to happen in our lives other than for apathy to settle in? It's a downward spiral and that is what Revelation 2:4 is speaking of: "You have abandoned the love you had at first." It's easy to lose that zeal and excitement for the things of God when He's not the object of our affection that we are chasing after.

In this letter, Jesus is speaking to the church in Ephesus. At one time these believers were known for their strong faith and deep love for Christ (see Eph. 1:15-16). But over time, things had changed. Their devotion and zeal for the Lord had shifted. The words of Revelation 2:4 illustrate just how far they had drifted. The Lord calls them out for abandoning their "first love." Girls, the truth is that whenever we feel distant from the Lord, we are the ones who have moved. He is still right there. We're the ones who've abandoned communion and relationship with Him and become apathetic. When we can recognize our apathy and repent of it before the Lord, we can be roused from the sin of apathy and can be a part of what God wants to do in our lives. So if you've abandoned the love you had for the Lord at first, God's heart and desire is for you to run wholeheartedly back to Him. Our religion and service aren't enough—God's wants our hearts fully surrendered to Him!

Return to Him...for He is your First Love. Never forget that!

DIY:

Re-Think (Journal & Pray):

+ Take some time to reflect on your salvation experience with Jesus. Journal your thoughts, the excitement that was there, the peace and hope you experienced in that time in your life.
+ For some of you reading this, you may be thinking to yourself that there has never been a time in your life where you've had a

salvation experience with the Lord. Maybe you've been "piggy-backing" on your parents' salvation experiences but you've never personally opened your heart to God's grace and surrendered your life to Him. If that is you, our prayer is that you would talk to your youth pastor, girls' minister, small group leader, or a parent and settle this once and for all. No games...just real talk here! You can't regain excitement for something that you never had in the first place. Our prayer is for every girl that goes through this book to have a growing, personal relationship with Jesus Christ.

✦ If you're at a place where the Holy Spirit has convicted you of living an apathetic faith, confess that before the Lord. Cry out to Him and return to your First Love.

Re-Visit the Word:

✦ Revelation 2:4
✦ Memorize: Romans 12:11

Re-Claim:

After going through today's junk of apathy, if you have realized you need a personal relationship with Jesus Christ, use this time with your parents, small group, youth pastor, or mentor and begin today to walk with Jesus.

In small group or with your accountability partner, discuss ways that you can hold each other accountable to fight against spiritual apathy. Take some time together to pray about your spiritual zeal.

Dream about what God will do through your group as you all truly get on fire and excited about making an eternal impact!

Day Two

JUNK: SELF-CENTEREDNESS

> Do nothing out of selfish ambition or vain conceit, but in humility consider others better than yourselves. Each of you should look not only to your own interests, but also to the interests of others. **Philippians 2:3-4** (NIV)

It's almost impossible to watch TV or listen to the radio without being bombarded by advertisements that appeal to and feed our selfishness. Now, before you start defending yourself and thinking that's not you, let me remind you that we still have a flesh bent toward selfishness. These ads appeal to us with "you deserve what you want" and "you can have it all" kinds of slogans. They also spend time and money promoting falsehoods like "you deserve to be happy so do whatever you want to get there." Although they are in direct conflict with Scripture, the ad campaigns apparently are successful, and unfortunately, even believers are buying into their philosophy.

Think about it. When was the last time you had a similar thought? Or even one like this: "If you don't look out for yourself then no one else will." You see, we live in a world that teaches us to be all about ourselves. The world rewards those who focus on self—not on others. This mindset is completely opposite of the counter culture theology of Scripture that tells us to put others before ourselves.

Why do you think that is so hard for us to do? Part of it is because our flesh is at war with the Holy Spirit inside us. When we submit to the Spirit, we become stronger spiritually; when we feed our flesh, it grows stronger. Giving in to your selfish inclinations will douse the fire of the Spirit in you. If you choose to give in and do whatever you want then your excitement and passion for God will diminish.

In order to feed the fire of God in you it is wise to follow the words of Jesus Himself who said in Luke 9:23, "If anyone wants to come with Me, he must deny himself, take up his cross daily, and follow Me" (HCSB). It's simple. DENY yourself. TAKE UP your cross daily. FOLLOW Jesus. Believers have always been called to be set apart—the same is true for you. Your choice. Feed self and reap the consequences. OR, let the Spirit of God lead you to a passionate life of selflessness.

DIY:

Re- Think (Journal & Pray):

+ What are some areas you have been acting selfishly in lately?
+ What consequences have you experienced from feeding your selfish nature?
+ How would you rate your passion for God right now?
+ Confess to the Lord the ways you have given yourself priority over the Holy Spirit and over other people.

Re-Visit the Word:

+ Memorize: Luke 9:23

Re-Claim:

In small group or with your accountability partner, discuss the following: What ways do you need to deny yourself? What does it mean to "take up your cross daily"? Where do you need to be "following Him" instead of following yourself?

Day Three

JUNK: INSECURITY

> But you are a chosen race, a royal priesthood, a holy nation, a people for His possession, so that you may proclaim the praises of the One who called you out of darkness into His marvelous light. **1 Peter 2:9** (HCSB)

Are you weighed down from feeling inadequate when you're around certain people? Have you found yourself so busy trying to measure up to some undefined standard of what you're suppose to be that it's left you feeling like you'll never measure up? Whether girls, and even women, want to admit it or not, insecurity plagues all of us! Some girls deal with this issue to a greater magnitude than others, but the bottom line is we all have moments in our lives when we feel insecure.

I believe wholeheartedly that when we can grasp our value and security in who He says we are, not who we should be or who we are striving to be, but who we ARE...that's the moment when everything changes. Girls, we've got to get over the mentality of thinking that these verses are cliché because they are truth from the Word of God, and we can stand on it and believe it for our lives. No matter who you are or what you've done, where you've been or what you've gone through in this life, as a follower of Jesus Christ, you are a daughter to the King of Kings. And it's time that we draw gentle strength and beautiful confidence from that truth and live like it!

The Bible teaches us that from the very beginning of time He knew us (Ps. 139:13-14). He set us apart before we were even born (Jer.

1:5). He knows all the days of our lives before one of them came to be (Ps. 139:16). He has a plan for us and we find our hope and future in Him (Jer. 29:11). He created us with a deep longing to love and to be loved, and yet He waits patiently for us to be fulfilled in Him. He loves us with an everlasting love (Jer. 31:3). He has clothed us in the garments of salvation and wrapped His robe of righteousness around us (Isa. 61:10).

And, girls, He has CHOSEN us to be royalty with Him, to proclaim praises to the One who has called us out of darkness and into His marvelous light (1 Pet. 2:9). Most importantly, and this is a truth that we obviously forget so often, we were created in the image of God (Gen. 1:27)! This truth alone is HUGE!

Wow, take a moment and let that sink in! I'm pretty sure that if got to the point where we didn't just read these words of truth but actually believed them, our lives would look a tad bit different than they do now, especially in our insecurity. When we see how He views us, we draw our worth and validation from the Giver of Life. It's time that we know and embrace who we are and glorify the Lord with this life we've been given.

God created you to be your own person—to be unique. He even created you with your own set of fingerprints. He knows how many hairs are on your head. And He has the days of your life planned out. He's got this! It's time to quit running the "rat race" of trying to live up to some standard you will never attain and embrace the girl God created you to be! Embrace who you are and quit trying to mimic the look and behavior of the next girl—be you! I pray you embrace all of who you are—the good, the bad, and the ugly—and live a life of authenticity that is contagious to those around you! It's the character of God and who He is, that gives you security and self-worth, not anything you can do on your own!

DIY

Re-Think (Journal & Pray):

+ After reading today, what issues of insecurity do you deal with in your life? Read 1 Peter 2:9 again and ask yourself, "What does this verse say about me"?

- Make a list of the things that you build your identity around. What things "define" who you are? (i.e.: sports, talent, grades, looks, boyfriend, popularity, family, reputation, accomplishments, friends)
- We base our identity on so many things other than on the One who created us. So looking at your list, ask yourself this question: "If I lose all of these things from my life, who am I?" Journal any thoughts that come from that exercise. Pretty convicting, huh?
- Do you truly believe that you were created in the Image of God? When you let that sink in, how can you begin to live with a holy confidence that shines from the inside out? Do you even want this transformation in your life? If so, then ask Him to help you embrace your God-given identity in Jesus—that He SO desires you possess!

Re-Visit the Word:

- 1 Peter 2:9
- Psalm 139: 13-14
- Jeremiah 1:5
- Psalm 139:16
- Jeremiah 29:11
- Jeremiah 31:3
- Isaiah 61:10
- Genesis 1:27
- Mark these verses in your Bible and allow the Holy Spirit to use them to shatter the insecure image you have of yourself. Let these truths transform your heart and mind.

Re-Claim:

In small group or with your accountability partner, discuss the ways you define the word insecurity. Do you find it hard to just be yourself in life? Why or why not?

Read and discuss the passages in the Re-Visit the Word section. Which is the hardest one for you to believe? Look up 1 John 3:1. Memorize this verse this week as a group—hold each other accountable to not only memorize this passage but believe it!

Day Four

JUNK: DEPRESSION

> I have seen all the things that are done under the sun; all of them are meaningless, a chasing after the wind. **Ecclesiastes 1:14** (NIV)

Read Ecclesiastes 1:14. Can you relate to the feeling that everything is meaningless? Have you ever felt like what you were doing was about the same as chasing the wind—which would be pointless? Understand this. Solomon, the writer of this passage, was a wise, wealthy king, and even he felt hopeless at times. That could be you. Maybe you've been down about something that's gone wrong with a relationship or a bad grade or even a bad look in the mirror. It can be anything that gets us to focus on the negative and forget that God has it under control.

It always breaks my heart to hear about someone committing suicide. I wonder how they could have gotten to the point where they felt that dying was the answer. I always wonder whether something could have been done to prevent such a drastic action. Many, many times people who choose to give up on life have been dealing with depression in some form. The more that I talk to people about depression, the more I recognize that it is not a respecter of persons and can strike anyone at just about any time. In Scripture there are a couple of different examples of people who dealt with depression in some way. You've just seen what Solomon wrote, and if you read the story of Elijah you can see how someone who was on top of their game suddenly plunged into negativity, isolation, and depression.

For his story, read 1 Kings chapters 18-19—this is one of my favorite stories and there are some things we can learn from Elijah that apply to today's "junk."

One thing to recognize is that depression can strike you even when things seem to be going your way. Elijah isolated himself out of fear and that is something that most people dealing with depression do— isolate. But here's the deal—isolation is for contagious diseases NOT Christians! You NEED fellow believers, so instead of withdrawing, seek help. Let people know what's happening with you and get some prayer support going.

We also tend to keep feelings of depression hidden. Psalm 42:5 says, "Why am I so depressed? Why this turmoil within me? Put your hope in God, for I will still praise Him, my Savior and my God" (HCSB). These words were written thousands of years ago proving that this is not a new issue for us as human beings. The psalmist's words point to the reality that we are emotional beings and can get overwhelmed in the wake of our circumstances. In fact, if you keep reading past verse 5 all the way through verse 11 of Psalm 42, you will catch a glimpse of the emotional roller coaster he experienced. Most of us can relate to that feeling of up and down when it comes to our emotions.

Just like in this psalm, God invites you to cry out to Him when you feel discouraged or depressed. If you continue to hide your true state of mind then you are allowing the enemy to take root in your life, giving him influence over your emotions. Girlfriend, God wants the best for you and that can only be found in Him. Expose the lies of the enemy for what they really are and deal with depression according to the TRUTH of Scripture. You are NOT alone—God is right there with you, and He is able to carry the weight of your emotions.

DIY:

Re-Think (Journal & Pray):

+ When was the last time you felt like something was meaningless?
+ Where does depression tend to start in your life?

+ What can you do to stop depressing thoughts as they form? (Check out 2 Cor. 10:5.)
+ Write out a prayer of thanksgiving that Jesus wants the best for you and that He defeats even the thoughts the enemy whispers in your head.

Re-Visit the Word:

+ 1 Kings 18-19 (Elijah's story)
+ 2 Corinthians 10:3-5

Re-Claim:

In small group or with your accountability partner, discuss the following: What ways can you bring light to your dark or depressing thoughts? How can memorizing 2 Corinthians 10:5 come in handy when you start to listen to the lies of the enemy? What role does Scripture play in shedding light? Are there areas of your life that need to be exposed to the light of Truth?

JUNK: BURNOUT

"So we must not get tired of doing good, for we will reap at the proper time if we don't give up." **Galatians 6:9** (HCSB)

Some of you may look at today's "junk" and blow it off, thinking it isn't an issue you deal with. But the truth is, burnout is an issue of life in any area. If you haven't already encountered it, it's coming. It's important to recognize the warning signs, know what to look for, and be ready to prevent it. There are two different kinds of burnout that can occur in the life of a believer that keep us from living our true identity in Jesus. First, burnout can occur from exhausting yourself from all the "religious" things you feel like you have to do for God to love and fully accept you. Your desire to do great things for the Lord in order to feed your need for approval makes you a person who never says "no" and agrees to do and be everything to everybody. You're simply wiped and exhausted. When you get to this place, even if you've had the best intentions, Satan has you defeated.

Second, burnout can occur when sin is not dealt with. You've drifted far away from the Lord, feeling burned out on the idea of even caring about the spiritual matters in your life. You'd rather live a carefree life where you call the shots than care about the life that God wants you to live for Him. When you live a spiritual life of defeat, burnout is inevitable. You throw your spiritual life aside out of pure emotional exhaustion and drift to a place where you begin to question God's goodness and would rather cling to the things that are tangible rather than cling to the One you cannot physically see. Read 2 Corinthians 4:18: "So we do not focus on what is seen, but on what is unseen. For what is seen is temporary, but what is unseen is eternal" (HCSB). This is a powerful reality. We must take some time to slow down and reflect on our lives, clinging to the faith and promises of God, trusting that He is good no matter what. He is in control and has a plan, even when things aren't easy or comfortable, even when we are walking through hard times.

Girls, we can't just tap out and give up on God when times get hard or when we are exhausted and stressed out with life. We've got to revive the excitement of our faith and continue running this race with perseverance. We must not tire of doing good. Galatians 6:9 says, "At the right time we'll reap a harvest IF we do not give up" (NIV). We've got to view this spiritual journey not as a race, but pace ourselves as if we're running a marathon. And the most important thing for us to understand is that burnout usually occurs from what we "do" for God. In order to avoid burnout in our lives, we need to shift all our energy and excitement into simply knowing Him. When we are pursuing Jesus through prayer, His Word, and worship, the passion will come from a heart transformed by Him.

In order to revive this excitement for Him and avoid spiritual burnout, we need to get back to the basics of knowing Him.

DIY:

Re-Think (Journal & Pray):

+ Do you recognize any signs of spiritual, or even physical, burnout in your life? What are some things you can do to safeguard your life from experiencing burnout?
+ Have you found yourself more concerned with "doing" things for God more than simply "knowing" Him?
+ Do you have a hard time saying "no," even to the good things? You must be willing to say no at times in order to prevent burnout.
+ Take some time to recharge your battery and carve out some time for rest.

+ Memorize: Galatians 6:9
+ 2 Corinthians 4:18

Re-Claim:

In small group or with your accountability partner, discuss the following: What do you think your motives are behind wanting to do "good things" for God? Do you see any warning signs of burnout, either spiritual or physical, in your life? What steps do you need to take to carve out time to rest before it gets out of control? What does it look like to find rest in the Lord?

HEALING BROKENNESS:

Burnout is something very real, and very damaging, to a church body. It is caused by excessive and prolonged stress and often happens in people who are constantly consumed with work or school and do not get much of a break. We have something in the counseling world called self-care, and it is crucial to maintaining a life of servant leadership. If you want to be someone who others can depend on, someone who can minister to others and someone who is constantly pouring out to others, then understanding the principle of self-care will enable you to avoid burnout and not give up before God has moved you!

"Never be lacking in zeal, but keep your spiritual fervor, serving the Lord," Romans 12:11 (NIV).

Practical steps to avoid burnout:
+ Be sure that you are taking care of yourself so that you can minister to others.
+ Get around godly mentors and leaders who can pour into you so you are not the only one pouring out.
+ Have a daily quiet time with the Lord so you are using God's strength not your own.

+ At the end of a tough day, give your burdens to Jesus. Lay them at the foot of the cross, and try not to take other people's drama home with you!
+ Make sure your schedule includes things that you like to do for fun: hanging out with friends, shopping, manicures, reading, etc!
+ Set boundaries!
+ Nourish your creative side through art, music, drama, etc.

Burnout can occur when you are overworked and overtired, so be sure to make taking care of yourself a priority and rest when necessary! Learning how to set appropriate boundaries is a skill, one in which we all could use a little help in!

salvaging
MY IDENTITY

WRAP-UP

+ What has been the most significant truth you've learned through this 40 day experience in this book and from God's Word?
+ How has the Holy Spirit begun transforming you, your thoughts, or the way you view yourself?
+ What areas of "junk" have actually been stripped from your life? What are some cool stories from your personal time with the Lord in the Re-Think section of the DIY?
+ How can you apply what you've learned from this book and re-produce these principles, maybe investing in someone else?

Remember that this journey of "salvaging your identity" is not an overnight process. The 8 projects covered in this book are issues we must strive to work on over the course of our lives. We will never "complete" all these projects or have it all figured out, but we must take action and fight to salvage the identity that the enemy and our culture are out to destroy...the identity that Christ died to give us!

Discussion Guide

RE-HASH WEEKLY MEETING AND DISCUSSION GUIDE

Hold weekly meetings to re-hash the material covered each week. Use the suggestions in this section for additional illustrations.

INTRO SESSION Getting Started

+ As an illustration, bring an old picture frame, wooden box, or other small inexpensive item that needs some TLC to be restored to beautiful.

+ Discuss what the problem with the item is and what needs to be done to make it functional and beautiful. Talk about seeing the potential and looking below the surface to see what it can become. You can also pull up some Pinterest pics to discuss what it looks like to take something from junk to treasure. Refer to the item you brought and ask: How can this be used?

+ Discuss how this item may have gotten to its current state. Imagine out loud what it may have been in its glory days and what purpose it might have served. Ask girls to consider how much was spent on it originally and then discuss how it might have gotten here.

+ Share about how we are so much like the item—designed and created to bring God glory in His purpose. Yet are we? Or do we feel more like the worn down, discarded, weather-beaten, tired-looking garage sale material?

+ Share that through this study we will learn how to take back and salvage our identity that the enemy has been tearing down and misleading for so long.

+ Give out books and go over the FAQs found in the "How To" section (pgs. 10-11). Help girls understand how each section works and how it relates to the salvaging theme.

CHAPTER 1 Project: Rescue Identity

+ Display a map on your phone or computer, or use an actual paper map.
+ Ask: What are maps used for?
+ Point out that you need to know where you want to go but also need to know where you are.
+ Stress that you can't know how to get where you want to go if you don't know where you are.
+ Discuss all the implications that girls bring up as they consider what this means from a spiritual standpoint.
+ Discuss the questions from "Re-Claim" section in each day's DIY.

CHAPTER 2 Project: Reclaim Reputation

+ **Video Option:** Show a clip from the show *Pawn Stars* or describe one in detail.
+ Explain the premise behind pawning items. (You take an item to a pawn shop and pawn it or sell it for less than its value because you want money at the time. You get a claim ticket that allows you to buy it back, but if you never redeem the ticket, you have sold your item for less than its value and missed out.)
+ Share that many of us have pawned our reputation to the world for much less than we are worth, and Jesus is standing here offering to buy it back for us if we will trust Him.
+ Discuss with girls that they must be willing to put in the elbow grease and effort that it takes to reclaim their reputation. It will require perseverance and willingness to press through the tough times in order to fully reclaim their reputation and use it the way God wants them to.
+ Discuss the questions from "Re-Claim" section in each day's DIY.

+ Show up for the meeting with no makeup. Bring makeup remover wipes to challenge everyone to join you in getting real, even to the point of being without makeup.
+ **Video Option:** Share the Dove commercial (search "Dove Evolution" on the Internet) that shows all the airbrush work that goes into a model. Emphasize that the standards we strive for are not realistic.
+ Stress that we need to create and be part of environments that embrace realness and where you feel safe even if you are feeling far from perfect. Explain that this group is that kind of place.
+ Discuss the questions from "Re-Claim" section in each day's DIY.

+ Bring a laptop or point to a computer for this illustration.
+ Ask: What are default settings? (Give the example of logging into your computer or laptop.) What is your default page? (Display your own and show them what your default home page is.) How does the computer know to go to that page? (Because you chose to set it to that default.)
+ Discuss how each person's life has some default settings. We are born with a sin nature and our default setting is to rebel against God. Only through salvation can our default settings be rebooted. We are given a new nature but still struggle with desires of our flesh. We must choose daily to submit our will to God and let Him control our settings.
+ Ask: When you want to change your default home page on the computer, how do you do it? (Go in to the settings, make changes, then save the new settings.) Say: Unfortunately changing our spiritual settings is not that simple. We must be intentional every morning and choose to override our old default setting of selfishness and let God take control through His Holy Spirit. It isn't a one time fix like a computer, but the more we submit control to God, the easier it becomes.
+ Discuss the questions from "Re-Claim" section in each day's DIY.

+ Do something as a group that has to do with a fitness challenge. You can go on a walk, lift some weights, put in P90X or other fitness video, CrossFit exercise routines online, or anything else physical.

+ Discuss how easy it is to exhaust ourselves physically and feel weak. Talk about how we can also feel weak spiritually and emotionally.

+ Ask: What causes that kind of weakness? How do you build strength physically? (regular exercise, pushing your muscles, practice, eating right to fuel your body) So, how do you build strength physically and emotionally? Why is it important for us to be stronger spiritually? Why do we often settle for spiritual weakness when we don't for physical weakness?

+ Discuss the questions from "Re-Claim" section in each day's DIY.

+ Create a tranquil, spa-like environment with low lights, peaceful music, good smells, etc. Consider doing hand massages or neck rubs to elaborate the illustration.

+ Ask: Why are times like this so special? (Peaceful, recharging.)

+ Share that our world is so crazy with pace, pressure, and expectation that peace is a hard thing to find.

+ Ask: What does retrieve mean? (Retrieve is to go get something and take it back.)

+ Explain that God offers us peace, but we have to be willing to embrace it. You must take the time to sit with God and let His peace surround you. You must also eliminate as many distractions as possible as you make this time with Christ your top priority.

+ Before the session, set an alarm on your phone to notify you during the small group time. Use a phone reminder as an example of what lengths you will go to when you don't want to miss something. Point out that when you are sick, getting to the doctor is important and you don't miss that appointment. Reinforce that the same should be true spiritually.

+ Explain that we are sick with the junk of the world we are dealing with and need the real Physician. He offers to make us well. Help them understand that we must seek Him and embrace His healing.
+ Discuss the questions from "Re-Claim" section in each day's DIY.

CHAPTER 7 Project: Recapture Devotion

+ Provide a blank piece of paper for each person. Instruct girls to tear out the shape of a heart.
+ Ask: What do you love? (Allow them to answer. Then emphasize that it isn't bad to love people/things, but the problem comes when our love for these people/things takes us away from our devotion to the Lord.)
+ Bring up something that is loved, like a friend and explain that there isn't anything wrong with loving other people except when it pulls us away from Christ. Say: Trouble arises when you love your friend so much that you do whatever they ask even when it compromises your integrity. (After this statement, tear out a piece of the paper heart you made.)
+ Say: Maybe you are on a sports team—there's nothing wrong with loving your team UNTIL you start devoting so much time to that team that you skip time with the Lord. (After this statement, tear another little piece of the paper heart.) Call on girls to give some other examples of how things they love can steal their devotion to the Lord. Instruct them to tear out pieces of their paper heart with each example.
+ Ask: How would you relate this heart experiment to the concept of recapturing your devotion for the Lord? (Explain that we are all passionate people, but when our passion is directed away from God it feels as if a piece of our hearts is missing.)
+ Ask: How do we redirect our passion where it is meant to be—on the Lord?
+ Discuss the questions from "Re-Claim" section in each day's DIY.

+ Gather around a wood-burning fireplace, bonfire, or fire pit. Light a fire and invite girls to look into the flames and think about the power that is there. Refer to some of the info in the intro section of this chapter.

+ Ask: Who do you know that really seems to be on fire for the Lord? What characteristics do they have that makes them that way? If fire represents the Holy Spirit, what part of the fire do you best relate to right now—the ashes, the coals, the smoldering log, the smoke, the scent, the flames? Why?

+ Discuss the questions from "Re-Claim" section in each day's DIY.

+ Wrap up this 8-week experience. Share that as part of Project: Rescue Identity, Day 1 (Acceptance), they were challenged to draw a picture and make a list of descriptive terms that represented their identity at that time. Instruct the group to look back at that journal page and read over their descriptions to themselves. As people are willing, invite them to share what has been the biggest change they have experienced over the last 8 weeks.

+ Read John 10:10 out loud. Mention that we have used this verse before and stress that the enemy is the one behind our identity theft. Only the Lord can help us salvage our identity and give us the life we long for.

+ As girls are ready, challenge them to tear the picture from the book and destroy the description of their previous identity. Encourage them to say the following out loud: "I refuse to let anyone steal what Christ died to give me, and I am choosing to salvage that identity and live the abundant life for His glory!"

+ Celebrate the progress the girls have made during this 8-week experience. Challenge girls to never stop salvaging their identity!

Journal your thoughts...

Sources

1. "Eating Disorders Statistics," last modified 2013, *http://www.anad.org/get-information/about-eating-disorders/eating-disorders-statistics/.*

2. Brene Brown, *Daring Greatly* (New York: Gotham Books,2012).

3. "Christians: More Like Jesus or Pharisees?" The Barna Group (www.barna. org), April 30, 2013, *https://www.barna.org/barna-update/faith-spirituality/611-christians-more-like-jesus-or-pharisees#.Uh5uGBao_7M,* used by permission.

4. Stephen Bramer and Kenneth Gangel, *Holman Old Testament Commentary - Genesis* (Nashville: Holman Reference, 2003).

5. "Eating Disorders Statistics."

6. "Facts on American Teens' Sources of Information About Sex," last modified February 2012, *http://www.guttmacher.org/pubs/FB-Teen-Sex-Ed.html.*

7. Matt Ferner, "Craig Scott, Columbine Massacre Survivor, Revisits The High School And Remembers His Murdered Sister Rachel Scott," The Huffington Post, April 10, 2013, *http://www.huffingtonpost.com/2013/04/10/craig-scott-columbine-mas_n_3054909.html.*

8. Dorothy Patterson and Rhonda H. Kelley, eds., *Women's Evangelical Commentary: New Testament* (Nashville: Holman Reference, 2006), 864-865.

9. Brian Mills and Nathan Wagnon, *Checkpoints: A Tactical Guide to Manhood* (Colorado Springs: NavPress, 2012), 159.